THE PIER

Glimpses of My Exotic Life on Bone's Jax Beach Fishing Pier, 1972–1983

Eve Bates

We do hope you have enjoyed this book that was a gift to you. Please encourage others to read it. This book (and Eve Bates' four others) may be purchased through *Amazon.com*. All proceeds from the sale of her books go to a Memorial Fund at Rutgers University that Eve set up to honor her Lithuanian-American farming parents

Also by Eve Bates:

Sudiev! Good-bye!: Joys and Hardships of a Lithuanian Immigrant Girl (a parental biography)
My Speckled Tales and Other Dimensions (a collection of eclectic short stories)
More Speckled Tales (a collection of short stories)

Copyright 2014
ISBN:9781502469021

The Pier: Glimpses of My Exotic Life on Bone's Jax Beach Fishing Pier, 1972–1983
Eve Bates

Front cover: Aerial photo of Bone's Jax Beach Pier. Credited to *Ponte Vedra Leader*, courtesy of Jacksonville Beach Historical Society.

Dedicated to all men and women who love to fish.

Robert L. Williams, creator of the pier (l.), and his buyer, George Bone. Photo credit to John Woodhouse, *Ponte Vedra Leader*, courtesy of the Jacksonville Beach Historical Society.

Notes of Essence

Anonymous

The horse and mule live 30 years
  and know nothing of wine or beers.
The goat and sheep at 20 die
  and never tasted scotch or rye.
The cow drinks water by the ton
  and then at 18 is mostly done.
The dog at 16 cashes in
  without the aid of rum or gin.
The cat in milk and water soaks
  and then in 12 short years it croaks.
The sober, modest, bone-dry hen
  lays eggs for us, then it dies at 10.
The animals are strictly dry
  they sinless live and swiftly die;
But sinful, gin-ful, rum-soaked men
  survive for three score years and 10.
And some of us, the mighty few
  stay pickled till we're 102.

A Prayer by Author Eve Bates

Holy Spirit of our universe, we eternally thank Thee for our space, our daily sustenance, and creature comforts. We thank Thee for all living creatures that fly, swim, and graze. And especially for the finned varieties we love to catch.

CONTENTS

Notes of Essence vi
A Prayer by Author Eve Bates vii
Acknowledgments xii
Author's Note xiv
1 – Again and Again the Pier Draws Me 1
2 – About Northeast Florida 6
3 – Mr. George Bone 10
4 – My Duty on the Pier 16
5 – Signs of Deep Friendship 22
6 – The Morning of My Husband's Slipped Disc 23
7 – Ann Bone 30
8 – Ray Holt 36
9 – George Befriends the Wrong People 41
10 – Rogerson's Slurpee Story 45
11 – George Celebrates His Birthday 46
12 – Harry Firestone Now in George's Life 47
13 – Ralph Haack 49
14 – Poole Leaves with a Policeman 50
15 – Break-Ins 52
16 – Bobby Stacker 54
17 – Johnnie Hexton's Restaurant 56
18 – Ed Davis Opens the Restaurant 59
19 – Pier People 61
20 – Workers of Italian Descent 66
21 – Ed Davis 69

22 – World-Record Hammerhead	71
23 – Celebrities	107
24 – Bone's Sister Comes to the Pier	118
25 – George Pins a Visitor to the Deck	120
26 – The Kindergarten Class	122
27 – Horace and Olive Arrive	124
28 – Pier Personalities Thin Out	130
29 – Marilyn's Homeless Story	142
30 – The Handsome Visitor Was a Dangerous Felon	152
31 – Apparently the Perfect Crime	156
32 – The Bank Robbery	160
33 – Surfers and Their Unending Squabbles	162
34 – Venomous Attack on George	173
35 – The Davises Are Giving Up	175
36 – The Mascot's Day	178
37 – A Surfer Strikes	182
38 – The Runaway Barge Problem	185
39 – The End of Poole	192
40 – Rhonda's Rule	195
41 – George Departs	200
42 – Hurricane Floyd Ends Pier	203
Epilogue	204
Recipes	207
WONDRA'S FLORIDA FOLK CAKE	207
PARTY RED BEANS	208
VANILLA CREAM CHEESE PIE	209
BEER-BATTER FISH FRY	210

A QUICK FISH REPAST	211
APPLE FRITTERS	212
OUR PIER'S CRAB CAKES	213
About the Author	214

Acknowledgments

I am fortunate indeed to be the recipient of the energy of my two resourceful daughters, Evelynne Stoklosa and teZa Lord, as well as of author Aileen Q. Wietstruk and my hard-working freelance copy editor, Beth Mansbridge.

I'd also like to recognize members of my writing groups for their invaluable help:

Special thanks to Dr. Michael Sanders, for his medical talents; John and Anka Newmann, for their holistic massages and reflexology; and Dori Bozung, acupuncturist physician, who kept me healthy and thriving.

Sizeable bouquets to my Tuesday Night Writers Group, a delightful handful of serious, steady, punctual people who meet weekly to critique, cajole, and inspire each other to work harder in order to get published. Several have made it several times and several more are about to be published. These special Tuesday Nighters are: Drew Sappington, Marie Vernon, Claire Sloan, Kathy Delaney, Jim James, Jack Boyd, Ken Ceglady, Bernard Welsh, Ralph Voss, Mel Minson, Ray Feliciano, and Carol "C.J." Goodwin.

Also, the Professional Writers Group, which meets every first Thursday at 5:00 p.m., have helped me. Some of them are: Carol M. Welsh, Michael Ray King, Beth Mansbridge, Rik Feeney, Evy Bell, Rize Cole, Frank Consetino, John Cordasci, Nina Cordova, Dianne Ell, Anastasia Glukhova, Pat Grillo, Mary Jane Hayes, Bob Kahrs, Ivy King, Charlotte and Bob Kramer, Margy Lang, Jeff Marshal, Margaret Nicholson, Nancy Quatrano, Jan and Hank Racer, Allison Rose, Jeff Swesky, Stephen Vickers, and Valerie Warner.

My appreciation goes to Mike Boyer for his early interest in my work, as well as to Dr. Mike, my fishing companion.

Of course, much appreciation goes to my beloved Tale Tellers Guild of St. Augustine, who have heard many of my tales. This is the most enjoyable assemblage I have ever belonged to and I love each and every one of them: Nancy Avera, Natalie Baltrami, Shirley Bryce, Kaye Byrnes, Shirley Dunwoody, Joe and Betty Fell, Gail Garvey-Ponasky, Joseph Halpin, Mary Jane Harris, Carol Johnson, Margaret Kaler, Chris Kastle, Barbara Lynch, Terry McConnell, Gail Pflaster, Rita Saker, Drew and Sharon Sappington, Jane and Wayne Sims, Marianne Stein, Donna and Bob Stephens, Frank and Mary Lee Sweet, Tuila Hudson, and George Red Bear. A colossal hug of gratitude to each of them for the help they have given me over the past two dozen years.

Author's Note

My account of the decade or so within this book, 1972–1983, is only one person's perception, my own. However, the story about this pier could be told in countless other ways.

Bone's Jacksonville Beach Fishing Pier, these characters, and these events actually occurred. Much of my source material comes from journals I recorded during my years of employment there.

The words spoken within these stories have been recreated to the best of my recollection. I tried to make this time come back to life by presenting what I witnessed.

The main characters retain their original names while others are substituted due to my imperfect memory.

The George Bone family were "salt of the earth" types, good people, but poor business managers.

1 – Again and Again the Pier Draws Me

Never before did anything attract me as quickly or as deeply as Bone's Jacksonville Beach Fishing Pier. Here I was, only three days' newly relocated to Florida and I was walking a thousand feet out over the Atlantic Ocean for the third time. It certainly was not a totally new experience, for I had fished on little piers and big piers all around New England and as far south as Hollywood, Florida, as well as from the world-renowned Steel Pier in Atlantic City, New Jersey. But this pier in Jacksonville Beach, referred to as Jax Beach, drew me like a honeybee is drawn to nectar. I felt like a goddess with god-like privileges to walk out onto the edge of the Atlantic Ocean.

It's mostly because my family and seafood are good friends, but also it was due to the endless string of characters I met while fishing there. I really loved that part of it. The people who frequented the pier were mostly of a different breed from the kind of folks I had seen in past days. I had adored working with lawyers and bankers, and the customers generally appeared appropriately dressed in my real estate office up in Clifton Park, New York. On this pier, people came to fish and to visit, and sometimes their manner of dress was difficult to understand. Granted most of them dressed for comfort, yet this observer is certain that some were clad in things strictly to be noticed, which baffled me, for many were definitely not comfortable.

I saw some strange idiosyncrasies concerning attitudes of dress and behavior there. For instance, I saw young couples not only wearing gold earrings, but also rings and studs in their eyebrows, noses, and lips. It was a new fad. When I commented on their sparkling jewelry, one bold young man spoke up and said he also had a gold ring in the foreskin of his member.

"Whoa!" I exclaimed. And, honest-to-god, that kid offered to exhibit it; I wasn't *that* interested.

One time a man appeared wearing heavy leather sandals and a thick, long, brown monk's robe and put in to fish beside me. I thought he was a real monk on vacation to fish in the Atlantic Ocean. Later I discovered he was only dressed that way for publicity, because he ran a bar in St. Johns County named The Monk's Vineyard. I thought that was really comical. We saw a never-ending parade of interesting getups.

I honestly think I went there because the pier was simply close to my new home, and it didn't cost an arm and a leg to use. All the rest was an intriguing surplus.

I love to fish from the surf, like I did when we lived in New Jersey. Gosh, there is no better feeling than to drag a nice seafood specimen like a sea trout out of the surf. But during wintertime in Northeast Florida, when the trade winds rattle in from the northern corners, getting your feet and legs wet in the surf is not good because of chilblain. Casting a line from the comfort of a bridge or pier is much better. Because the fee was only a dollar, I quickly fell in love with Bone's Jax Beach Fishing Pier (hereafter referred to as Bone's Pier). Anyway, this is my reasoning for frequenting this pier so often.

...

So far, I had been admitted to the pier by employees. Today I met another pair of engaging people. The pier's owner, Mr. George Bone, received me at the tackle shop and we exchanged pleasantries.

I said, "Hello, Mr. Bone, I'm glad to meet the captain of this ship." I told him I was a new arrival, a tomato farmer from New Jersey, and hoped to catch a lot of fish from his pier.

He flashed me a charming smile and said that depended on my ability to catch a fish and that the ocean was known to have a "bunch of 'em."

I walked away smiling and thinking how much Mr. Bone looked like Errol Flynn, the renowned Hollywood actor; he had the same beautiful mannish face and twinkling blue eyes. Not a thing showed up to pinpoint any difficult personality problems on this first encounter.

At the first slough, I saw a man pulling up a big fat whiting, and I thought, *Uh-oh, the fish are right up here in the shallow surf.* So I decided to put in beside him, and there is where I first met Mr. Robert L. Williams, the founder of this pier. When he noticed I was not clumsy with the casting and not a threat to his pastime, he became friendly. However, from the way he spoke, I knew he was wishing he still owned the pier. With my habit of questioning people I quickly learned it was his opinion that Mr. Bone was not the businessman he thought Mr. Bone would be. What he said out of the blue that day, made me wonder.

"Do you see these dark, splintery planks that catch our feet as we walk over them?" he asked with a bit of fire on his tongue.

"Yes. As a matter of fact, I just tripped over there," I said, and pointed to a terribly rough place in the deck where I hopped, skipped, and jumped so as not to fall.

"As you can plainly see," he said, "there are spots on this pier in need of repair. The annual storms from the Northeast beat the heck out of piers down here. What burns the tar out of me is the fact that December, January, and February is the time of year to be at work at repairing these damages. He waits till after spring arrives, when the weather gets warm and fishermen jam this place again."

I had to agree with this man's premise, but still I thought the other guy must have his legitimate reason for his hesitation.

"Maybe Mr. Bone doesn't have the cash flow for such a project?" I suggested.

"Well, I had this pier for eight years and I know what comes in over that counter in there. True, there is no profit here during January or during weeks when it's cold because not enough people come out. But when it gets warm there's more than enough made for upkeep needs." Mr. Williams was agitated but seemed relieved to share his annoyance of that moment with someone.

"What's his problem?" I asked courageously.

"I don't know," Williams said sadly, "but he certainly does have difficulties, and if he doesn't pay better attention to what's going on around here, pretty soon that problem will do him in."

I was shocked to hear such sadness. For a moment I began to think that Williams was a rakish man who thought nothing of putting a fellow citizen down before every stranger he met. However, as I got to know more about him, I decided that Mr. Williams would not hurt anyone for any reason. He was simply uptight over the lack of care given to something of which he was quite fond, and had to share his feelings with a mature person. I happened to be handy.

...

   Mr. Williams was a self-made man. He was known to call himself a "gambler," but I think he was mostly a businessman. Born and raised on a North Carolina cotton and tobacco farm, he soon decided on other ventures. After some college courses, he worked for the state as a surveyor.
   When World War II broke out he went to work at the shipyard in Charlestown, South Carolina, where he narrowly escaped death by being accidentally imprisoned in the lower bowels of a new warship. His work as inspector took him crawling into every inch of the new keel to inspect riveting and marine welding of the ship's plates. A welder had arrived to his assignment, not knowing anyone was down in the hold. The welder struck his arc and proceeded to encase the inspector within the hull. Shortly after the noon hour, the keel was finished.
   Williams later explained that he did not panic for an hour or so because he thought workers would hear his pounding and he'd be free in no time. But because of the four to five thousand employees and the different noises they made at work, such as the punchers, shearers, acetylene cutters, electric welders, machine riveters, chippers, caulkers and such, nobody heard Williams' frantic knocking with his flashlight. The normal shipyard racket overpowered his attempt to be heard. His wife went out searching for him that night, to no avail, and she was left worrying what to do next. It wasn't till the next morning when workers came back to their jobs on the quay, and in the early-morning stillness someone heard the faint tapping from his only tool, his flashlight, and he was cut out of his deadly steel tomb, pronto.
   Williams and his family saw this as a divine revelation, and he feared little after this episode.

...

   After the war Williams decided to become a car dealer and opened a Ford agency in Scotland Neck, North Carolina. That did so well he opened a second agency in Rich Square, NC, and between the two he quickly made a million. That of course was during the mid-1950s when Henry Ford came out with those long, sleek V-8 models equipped with 85 horsepower. Williams didn't have to work to sell them—everybody wanted that *new look*. He said he had trouble keeping them in stock, so good was his business.

As an entrepreneur he had many employees and many new chores on his hands, and so he went fishing as often as he could get away. This is where he found true relaxation. He frequented the many new piers built along the east coast of North Carolina and discovered the owners were making a good return on their investments. And that is when he decided he too would build a pier and cut away from all the work of the dealerships.

He sold the agencies for a good profit and invested in building a steel-beamed pier which he named the Williams Steel Fishing Pier, in Virginia Beach, NC. He said he built this pier for under $200,000 and sold it for $100,000 profit. But before he decided on the exact location, he made a study of the surrounding environment. He went down to Jacksonville Beach, FL, and found three oceanfront lots for which he paid only $3,500! With fresh plans for a new pier and designs for a new home, he was ready to move his family farther south.

2 – About Northeast Florida

It got so Mr. Williams and I became frequent visitors at the pier. And while we sat waiting for the fish to bite, we sojourned a while. We discovered we both had traveled a bit and we discussed our experiences in Rome, Japan, and Australia. I told him my husband was in sales with the Bulova Watch Company, which had transferred us to Northeast Florida territory to establish a retail market with the area's jewelers. And because I was delighted to be here, I asked if he was happy winding up at Jacksonville Beach, Florida. He assured me there was no place better on God's green earth than right here.

"I can feel my heart healing as I sit here in the sun," he confided.

Right here, about an hour after the high tide, I felt a small nibble, and when I tightened up my line I found I had something big enough to command my full attention; our visit was ended temporarily. I felt jubilant for a minute or so, but it turned out to be a skate after my live bait.

"Shucks!" I screamed.

But that is how fishing is. One minute you might be dealing with a red drum and looking forward to an incredible seafood banquet, and the next minute you might have to tangle with a trash fish big enough to sap your strength.

"We never know," I said, "what we have until it is brought to the top of the water."

Mr. Williams laughed at my expressions, and then he finished his thoughts by saying, "Northeast Florida specifically attracted me. My wife and I made a three-day fact-finding trip around the Northeast before we invested here in Jacksonville Beach. This area has a great deal to offer my family, to my way of thinking. First of all because it is underdeveloped and because of its magnificent beaches, I predict Northeast Florida is in for a big boom in growth. This area is considered one of the six most important bio-diverse areas in this country. The variety of living things peculiar to this place is amazing."

"Really, Mr. Williams? What do you see here that is not found elsewhere in Florida or the Deep South?"

"Oh my goodness, quite a few. There are many key plants and known animal species. For instance, my wife was telling me about something called the white-topped pitcher plant and the panhandle lily, which are of interest to her collections. And, of course, I'm sure you have already seen the baby Florida manatee that was hanging around this pier for a few days this week looking around for its mother. The manatee is a mammal that breeds alive and suckles its young."

"I know. I was one of those that the manatee held eye contact with yesterday morning as it lay on top of the water looking up at us. But I didn't know the manatee was something special here."

"Yes, it is. We suspect that the mother of this young one was accidentally killed by a fast-moving boater, and the baby was stranded here until it went off on its own. We called Marine World and when they finally showed up, the baby had disappeared from our pier."

"What else do you think is unique to this area you chose to live in?" I was completely under Mr. Williams' spell.

"I suppose you have heard of Florida's snakes and its gopher tortoises, haven't you?"

"Oh, sure. Florida's diamondback rattlers are known all over," I said, trying to sound like I knew something about them when I knew little more than the fact that they belonged in Florida.

"I'm certain that most people are not aware how big some of these granddaddy rattlers can get to be—fifteen to sixteen feet long, in this particular place under the sun. I've seen a rattler with a head as big as a big man's hand. That size could knock a person down easily. I don't believe a child could get away from one that big. We are lucky this animal chooses to move out as we move into its habitat."

"Yes, sir," I agreed.

However, I immediately thought of the four-foot rattler found dead on the road, killed by traffic on A1A last night. I knew what he meant, though. Most wildlife move on farther when man comes into their habitat with bulldozers and other development tools, but I didn't want to let him think I wasn't with him.

"Anything else that you found of interest here?" I didn't want to let him go.

7

"In my yard in Ponte Vedra, I often see the red-cockaded woodpecker, rarely seen elsewhere in the country, and a large black indigo snake makes his home in the wild hedges next door. These are Northeast Florida residents. And then I'm fascinated by the rivers and underground springs."

"Oh, I am too. I'm still looking for a small spring and its one-acre-sized pond, which Mrs. Wertenberg Smith of Haddonfield, New Jersey, introduced me to back in 1942 when we stopped for a rest somewhere on Interstate 10. We were on our trip from Daytona to Birmingham, Alabama. It was pretty far west of here. I haven't yet found it, but I think I will one day. I remember swimming in this tiny lake with an open hole way down in the earth, thirty feet below, with clear, cold water bubbling up out of that spring. I remember there was a very large catfish and some smaller ones hovering over the spring beneath me. It was fascinating!"

"Yes. There are no fewer than thirty springs of the first magnitude here in Northeast Florida. And each one discharges many millions of gallons of water each day. No other state or nation can rival this phenomenon. Underwater caves, limestone formations of sinks, ravines, underwater streams and rivers, and aquifer recharge areas are fascinating mysteries in this habitat. At least they are to me."

"But Mr. Williams, none of these things would affect your ocean fishing pier, would they?"

"Certainly. Sure it would."

"How would it affect your pier?"

"It would affect the people who built piers on a lakefront property more than it would affect me, but a close-by river was very important to my choosing a location for my fishing pier, and rivers are part of the area's water system."

"I understand what you're saying. And of course you are almost beside my all-time favorite river, the St. Johns, which is the only major river in the country that flows from south to north. I love this river, I really do," I told him with a tingle in my voice.

"Rivers of North Florida are relatively unspoiled," he told me. "And should be kept that way. They make the very important connection between upland habitats and those of us who live on the ocean's shores."

"Oh, I totally agree," I said. "I can't stand a river clogged with debris. St. Johns River is still full of fish and shrimp. I've been told that the river turns to a reddish hue when the red bass are migrating."

"One of the numerous river systems of Northeast Florida is this river, deep enough to support a busy deep-water harbor, and it flows northward, parallel with the eastern coast for three hundred miles before it drains into the Atlantic Ocean just a mile north of this pier. Let me tell you that I believe the river's closeness is the reason for some of our big catches. When the shrimp fleet returns to port, they clean out their nets and dump all their trash fish before they enter the harbor, and this, I do believe, brings in some of those big kings, cobia, and billfish looking for an easy dinner."

...

Here in 1960, Mr. Williams built the 1,200-foot-long fishing pier at Sixth Avenue S. for $81,000, and insured it through Lloyds of London with hopes he would never have to use the insurance. However, he did have to. On September 9, 1964, Hurricane Dora arrived here huffing and puffing like a wild thing and blew away a couple of hundred feet of the longest pier on the Atlantic Ocean at the time. The storm also stripped away mostly all of the siding from the pier's building and tore up the pier's decking considerably. The pier was rebuilt, ending at the T-shaped terminal, but minus the three-hundred-foot end, which took away its claim of "longest pier."

Williams said that because he had the experience with rust on his North Carolina pier, he decided to build the Jacksonville Beach landing using creosoted wooden pilings, which he drove down fifty to sixty feet deep to rest on hard pan. And because of this he thought the pier would stay for a long time, at least thirty years or more.

But nature has its fickle ways. Hurricane Dora's wicked performance created many unexpected problems for him. It took months to fix up and restore the post storm damages. Then, in 1967, Williams suffered a severe heart attack which, after eight years of pier ownership, necessitated that he refrain from problems of business. And that was when George Bone came into the picture.

3 – Mr. George Bone

Knowing of the boom going on in Northeast Florida, Mr. Bone arrived from his digs in North Carolina looking for work in construction. Mr. Williams liked this strong, healthy-looking man and hired him. Bone was handy, and he was an honest man. He gave an honest day's work and more. He was a big help to the stricken pier owner.

When Bone and his wife showed interest in ownership, Williams decided to make it easy for George to buy the pier. Mr. Williams made the deal with no down payment, and payments were arranged on the percentage of what the pier brought in each month. So the mortgage payment Bone owed in January was a lot lower than what he owed in July and August. The only thing Williams clearly emphasized was the clause that permitted him to fish without cost, as well as for members of his family.

All employees were to be notified of this. Bone and Williams shook hands, wished each other good luck, and Williams went home to plant his garden and regain his health.

...

Like his grantor, George Bone was also born to a tobacco-growing farmer. However, from stories he told me over a period of a decade, I could readily see that his beginnings were a lot less fortunate. The three boys and two girls were orphaned before they became of age. George was the youngest boy and, at twelve, had to assume care of his eight-year-old baby sister while the rest of the siblings went out to work to help make ends meet.

They stayed on the farm, but it wasn't easy, he said. When asked, he admitted that he was often hungry, with nothing in the house to eat. One of his aunts who lived close-by and supervised the Bone kids, contributed daily to their subsistence. She usually brought over a

Brunswick stew or a pan of cornbread. One day, he said, he and his little sister were so hungry that their beloved auntie suggested they suck on a couple of small stones to quell their hunger pains, until she made a stew for them. George first had to go out into the woods and shoot a couple of squirrels, and auntie had to find some beans, potatoes, or cornmeal before she could cook any kind of a substantial meal.

"Oh, how gooooooood that stew was!" he proclaimed from a vivid memory.

He laughed over his recollections of those faraway days, but I didn't think it was a bit funny, perhaps because I had never been that hungry. At my childhood home during the Great Depression we never had to eat squirrel; we had plenty of game at our home when I was a kid, but never squirrel meat. I don't know why. Perhaps my parents thought squirrels were too much like rodents and left them alone. Anyway, I felt myself feeling sorry for the Bone children and those past hardships they endured at such a tender age.

But George had a way to make people laugh. All he had to do was speak funny and with exaggerated conviction, and I thought he was a riot. He often imitated his beloved auntie who had looked in on him and his siblings. He imitated her in a feminine voice: "Sit down heah, young uns, and eat yo suppa."

George didn't have much education. As a matter of fact he said he didn't even graduate from grade school. Fortunately, he married a smart lady who was a high school graduate. I often wondered where he would have been without her. He depended on Ann's judgment a great deal, and she let him have his way much of the time.

I also wondered if George was able to read. One of the ways he made me laugh was his act of pretending to read something serious. He would hold the racing schedule upside down and make noises as if he were actually reading the script. But I don't ever recall seeing him reading a daily newspaper or one of the fishing periodicals.

At the age of fifty-five, mind you, he wasn't even faintly aware of how our democratic government worked. He never, ever had registered to vote. He had never served on a jury. He said he had never even looked at a *New York Times* newspaper or *The New Yorker* magazine. He was often negatively critical concerning elected officials. When I asked why he didn't care to vote so that he could help vote out badly chosen people and participate in his government, he silently walked away from our conversation. I'm not saying George was a dummy, but certainly he wasn't hip to a lot of things, either.

In 1973, he said, their small farm was still intact. Fortunately they had not lost it, thanks to the goodness of his kin, but they came close to doing so a few times. The oldest siblings kept up on the taxes. It turns out that presently his oldest brother was incarcerated on a charge of rape, and his second brother had suffered a severe heart attack and was living under a doctor's care. I knew that George felt deep sadness for his kinfolk, but he often talked tough, especially about the one sitting in prison.

I heard him say to Leaston, his visiting brother: "He belongs in a lockup. He did wrong. He deserves what he got!"

George was speaking to his brother about their dear oldest brother. Leaston nodded in agreement, but remained silent. These two younger ones visited each other often and took care of each other's needs. George always had a couple of his employees fishing for seafood to freeze for Leaston's household.

Perhaps it was a combination of their troubles that caused George and his sickly brother to befriend hard liquor. They both drank straight whiskey from eight-ounce water glasses and became stupid rather quickly early in the day. Soon after I arrived in Jacksonville Beach, George's young brother died from a fatal heart attack, and I noticed that when George came back from the funeral in North Carolina, he drank even heavier. He now began to choose friends who drank, and he had plenty of these who stopped by often, sometimes daily to kibitz, but mostly to have a snort with George.

....

The closest friend George had was Dick Poole. A couple of years older than George, Mr. Poole was a part-time worker and George's mentor on the pier. Tall, baby-faced and thin as a rail, he was a retired coastguardsman who first worked for Mr. Williams, and supposedly knew the pier business thoroughly. George often bragged how fortunate he was to have Mr. Poole on his side, because he knew everything there was to know and was no farther away than the telephone whenever a problem needed deliberation.

"I can't tell you how important Poole is around here," George told me early on. "I couldn't put a number on things he has done for us, and hasn't charged me a cent for his work."

I knew that he and George were real buddies. I had seen Mr. Poole warmly hug and kiss George on the cheek several different times, like a real brother would do. Poole did not have a brother, and when George confided family and business problems Mr. Poole seemed to genuinely empathize with him. I admired Poole for that, because poor George, who had lost two brothers, certainly did need a friendly touch now and then.

....

Richard Rogerson was another good friend. Richard was the only one who could tell George Bone to "Go home and sober up, for crise sake! You're making an ass of yourself!" And without a word, George obeyed him.

I saw a lot of Richard. He was our nearest neighbor on Second Street and he spent a lot of time on the pier. At the pier he was either working or fishing. Richard was an automotive teacher in the public school system and needed extra money. He was divorced, with three boys in college whom he was helping to support. He was recently remarried, to Muriel, also a teacher, and a lovely person to be around. They were happily awaiting a new baby. I liked this family very much.

One day Richard tapped at my kitchen window and asked if he could come in for a cup of coffee. He asked me to take over his part-time job at the pier since he was scheduled for open-heart surgery the following week.

I told him I was surprised as heck, because he looked so much like a man who was not only in good health, but also a man who was happy with life. Gosh, he was a good-looking soul, a lot like Hollywood's Gary Cooper, tall and beautifully muscled, and with tender southern manners.

"They told me I'd be as good as new after this surgery," he lamented, with a radiant smile on his sunny, deeply suntanned face.

"Yes, certainly," I told him, "I'll be glad to hold your job down, Richard, but maybe George wouldn't want me. Perhaps he'd prefer having a man behind that tackle shop counter."

"I've already spoken to him. As a matter of fact it was George who suggested I ask you if you were interested in this part-time work. He has observed that you know a lot about fishing, and he likes your personality. Please, Eve, take this job if you can," he actually begged me.

"Sure, Richard, I'll go up there a little after lunchtime, when Mr. Bone will be there, and I'll accept the job to help you out."

This seemed to please Richard, and he left smiling widely.

...

"Richard says you need help in the tackle shop. Can I help you out, George?" I asked as soon as I saw him the next morning. That's how I approached him for Richard's job.

George stood staring at me, not saying a word for the longest moment. I started to giggle because he seemed confused, so I began to talk about poor Richard and his big problem. After all, open-heart surgery back then was fairly new and was a big risk ….

Interrupting me, George said, "Yes, well, we'll start you off on a trial basis and see what you can or cannot do. Can you come in tomorrow morning at ten and work until one o'clock, and we will start you off."

And that is how it happened. I worked for Mr. Bone for the rest of the '70s, until we built a retirement home down in St. Augustine. At first it was the most enjoyable labor I had ever done. As far as I'm concerned, fishermen and fisherwomen are the best grade of people on God's earth. What a job!

I would have been glad to pay for the privilege of being up there, but every Friday morning Ann Bone paid me a few shekels by check. In no time George discovered I was worth more than the minimum wage of $1.60 per hour and hiked my pay every six months until I earned at least a hundred dollars a week, sometimes more, depending on the number of hours I put in. He always paid me in cash. I don't know if he paid everybody like that, or only the two part-timers. Many times I saw him give Dick Poole a twenty-dollar bill for two hours' work.

There was a big turnover with pier workers. The day after I was hired, George had just fired a young man who was hired only a month before. He was the early-morning opener. Dick Poole broke him in and showed him what had to be done early in the day. To me, it seemed like the man was a devoted worker.

"I just fired that SOB, and we are shorthanded around here," George complained.

"Why was Bucky fired?" I wanted to know.

"Because the SOB stole seventy-five dollars from me, that's why."

"How do you know he stole seventy-five dollars from you?" I asked.

"That SOB came in wearing a brand-new pair of cowboy boots, and I happen to know where he bought them, and I happen to know they cost seventy-five dollars, that's how I know it was him who stole my money!"

"Wowie," I said in a sympathetic tone, "I'm sorry you happened to hire a thief."

"We deal with all kinds of bastards around here. But I've noticed that you get along with everybody out there on the pier. I need someone like you around here. Are you sure that Linwood will let you work here?"

I knew George liked my husband since he had many times invited Linwood to have a drink with him.

"George, I have no reason to believe he wouldn't like that."

And, I thought, *if only you knew how much my husband enjoys the stories I bring home. Ha!*

4 – My Duty on the Pier

Mr. Bone told me I need not worry about counting the money at any time; he or Ann or Mr. Poole would take care of that part. He instructed me to pay strict attention to the cash register and the tackle shop's counter and its area because "there were people around looking for a chance to grab something." I thought he was being facetious, but I soon discovered he was not fooling.

I was told to keep my eye on a man by the name of Blackie Reasor because he was known to be a slick "taker" and a "borrower" who got away with all kinds of things without paying out cash. Although less than fifty years old, he lived on a meager disability check. Supposedly he had a bad back problem. Although he could work and often took small carpentry jobs around the neighborhood, he preferred not to work. He had a new young wife and a beautiful baby boy. Phyllis, his energetic second wife, worked in the pier's restaurant, and that was his reason for hanging around. He handed me his card one day. It declared: *No Phone; No Address; No Business, No Reports; No Traveling; No Complaints; Now Retired; When I have the urge to work, I lie down until the urge passes.* But he fished every day.

He and his family lived in a small second-floor furnished apartment across the street from the pier. Like all fish eaters, he was wiry and strong. There wasn't a thing he didn't know about how to catch fish; he'd had a lot of exposure to this sport. Despite Blackie's "taking" reputation, he was respected for his knowledgeable accomplishments and for catching more fish than anyone else on Bone's Pier. He bathed in this, his limelight. He attracted newcomers with his fishing skills and storytelling. He spoke through clenched teeth, and his Kentucky drawl was enrapturing.

On my very first day of employment, Mr. Bone showed me how to work the big, noisy cash register, and I was left alone because he was needed elsewhere. Blackie, who had been sitting on the front bench watching me getting my instructions, approached the counter and asked to see a "yellow Sea Hawk," a favorite lure for catching sea trout. I took the box of Sea Hawks out from the case below and placed it on the counter. The phone rang. I excused myself and turned to answer it. It was Tony Slack at the local radio station looking for the pier's daily report.

I said, "Good morning, Tony. Today, April 17, 1973, is a beautiful sun-splattered day at the beach this morning. It is currently seventy-two degrees, with an expected high of seventy-nine to eighty degrees this afternoon. The wind is from the south at five to ten miles per hour, and the humidity is 87 percent. The sea is quite calm, at two to four feet. It is soon coming up to high tide at eleven thirty this morning, and it will be low tide at 5:03 p.m. They are presently catching a few whiting and small drum out there. That's it. Have a good day, Tony. Bye-bye."

The entire message took a minute or less, and when I turned back to the counter, Blackie was walking away saying, "There is no yellow Sea Hawk, thank you."

I thought that was funny; I had just opened a fresh box of a dozen lures earlier that morning and there was usually a yellow lure among them. I dumped the box on the counter and counted out eleven lures, with the yellow one at the very bottom. Since I hadn't sold any yet, it looked like Blackie had palmed one on me, but it wasn't a yellow one.

"Yo, Mr. Blackie," I called to his backside as he was heading out to fish.

He ignored my call.

I tried again: "Yo, Blackie. Yooo-hoo, Blackie!"

But he ignored my voice.

I picked up the mike and turned it up. "Please come back here, Mr. Blackie, and pay for that black Sea Hawk."

Everyone on the pier and close to the pier now knew Blackie was in trouble with the new female clerk. Mr. Bone hurried back to the tackle shop and wanted to know what had happened.

"I hope nothing, yet," I told him, wishing the situation was still only between Blackie and me.

But Mr. Bone knew and he literally went straight for Blackie's jugular out on the pier. He took hold of Blackie by his neck and then let him go. Mr. Bone next grabbed up Blackie's stuff and brought it all back and put it inside the tackle shop: two fairly new reels, two new trout rods, and a tackle box filled with secret lures and other fishing paraphernalia. Blackie soon came in and paid me the two dollars for the black Sea Hawk. Because there were more blacks than any other color, I had guessed right on the color, but the boss was not aware of that fact. Mr. Bone kicked Blackie off the pier and told him he didn't want to see him ever again.

Blackie was back the next day, lounging as usual on the long bench with his morning coffee and his eyes on everyone's gear as they passed through the mall. But he never again tried to pull anything over on me after that first attempt.

And he knew George Bone would not permanently kick him off the pier. From that day, though, he knew he couldn't trust me to accommodate his ways.

There were other Blackie incidents at the pier. One day, as I approached the area where he lived across from the pier, he drove up with a boat carrier attached to his little black pickup.

"Look, Miss Eve," he yelled. "Look what a rich dude gave me this morning."

"That's a nice carrier," I said, "but you don't own a boat. What will you be doing with it?"

"I'll be selling it," he said with a laugh.

Blackie did sell the heavy carrier that same day. Somebody got a real good bargain. We were left to think of the poor fisherman who came in after a long day at sea and could not find where he had parked his carrier.

Another time, I saw Blackie with his hand bandaged.

"What happened to your hand?" I wanted to know.

"Aw, I had a little accident," he murmured.

Later I learned from his stepson, Daryl Sprague, that Blackie had shot off his finger while cleaning his gun. That story didn't click with me because Blackie was not a stupid individual. He was anything but stupid.

Another uncomfortable thing occurred early on in my pier life at Bone's. Although George had already told me that Mr. Poole was his best friend and second in command on the pier, it was mainly George who broke me in on the way to run his pier. George told me I was allowed to have two or three Pepsi's daily, but I never drank that stuff. And I was allowed to order a hamburger from the restaurant whenever I got hungry. But in all the time I was there I probably had only three or four hamburgers. I did have a bowl of hot grits every morning, whenever I had the early-morning shift. George was a generous soul.

George told me that when and if a known kid asked for a free pass to fish (a couple of kids sat right there on the front bench), I should ask them to help clean up the pier, and then allow them to fish for free. But never allow anyone on the pier without doing something to earn the privilege.

Early on, two boys who played hooky from school were on the pier practically every day. They were Joey Panclowski and "Red" Stevenson. Joey was about fourteen or fifteen and the poor kid had a nose bigger than Jimmy Durante's. He was always on the pier, it seemed. He was naturally very slow and gullible. He knew nothing about good fishing, as did other boys of his age. But he was a willing person to earn his way on the pier, and I had him sweep and clean up whenever he asked to fish for free. Red, on the other hand, knew a great deal about fishing and how to catch fish using certain bait and all that. So I used to ask Red to help me in the tackle shop when I ran into a busy period.

Around the time of my first month there, I had a customer who wanted new 20-pound test Ande line on his fishing rod, while I also had a lineup of seven or eight people waiting for bait and to be admitted to the pier. I spotted Red sitting on the long bench, waiting to ask me for permission to fish, so I beckoned for him to come to the tackle shop counter. I asked if he knew how to work the line machine. Red said, "Of course," and I asked him to come inside the tackle shop and string that man's reel, which Red obligingly did.

I had all the other people taken care of and was about to thank Red, when in stormed Mr. Poole and as he swung his way through the tackle shop's doorway he yelled out, "Why do you have these GD thieving kids in here?"

With both hands he forcibly banged into my breasts so hard I knew I would have black-and-blue bruises for a week or more—and he pushed me backward until, unbalanced, I crashed against the island counter of the tackle shop. Clumsily, he fell against me, but I wormed my way out from beneath his body. Mad as a stinging hornet, I grabbed that skinny man by a shoulder and leaned myself into him, pinning him against the cluster of hanging tackle.

With my free hand I put my fist against his nose with some force and I said, "Mr. Poole, I don't know what you're up to, but you have just hurt me. Listen to me, sir. Unless you want to taste my fist sandwich, don't you ever dare put your dirty hands on me ever again. Do you understand what I am saying?" And I gave his nose a good push.

I think because I had moved Mr. Poole's false teeth out of place, he definitely understood I would not stand for any of his attacks. Subsequently he became friendly towards me. He used to come up on the pier when I was on the early shift, and he would send me downtown to Jacksonville to pick up the racing forms. He and Baby, his wife, as well as Ann and George Bone used to frequent the dog races every Friday night. They liked to acquaint themselves with the program. Of course I gladly obliged him. I didn't know if Mr. Poole had discussed our wrestling match with George, but after that day I kept my eyes open around Poole.

…

When I first started, George had me come to work at ten or eleven o'clock to help out with the big morning rush. All I had to do was stand at the cash register and ring up the fees and stamp the fishermen and women and children with that day's date, fix them up with the bait they desired, and admit them to the pier.

The clerk who opened the pier for business at six o'clock in the morning in the summertime had much more physical work to do. First he opened the front door and, second, he raised the American Stars and Stripes on days it was not raining. He washed down the pier's outside toilet. Then, if there was an early delivery of bait, usually in one-hundred-pound ice chests, he spent the time not needed at the register in packing the bait into one-half-pound bags for the freezer.

We always received a dozen or so telephone inquiries. People wanted to know the condition of the water—if it was clear or muddy—what phase was the tide, and what, if anything, was caught so far that day. Once a week the new merchandise arrived and had to be sorted and hung on their proper hangers and pegs. These were the pegs and spindles which Mr. Williams had put up to accommodate various sizes of swivels, one- and two-hook fishing tackle, various sizes of fishing line, and lead weights. When George found out I could handle the opening shift, I helped with that. His counters and glass cases were never so clean and shiny.

One day my husband came up to have lunch with me at the pier. When George spotted him, he took Linwood aside and I heard him telling my husband what a good person I was and what a good worker he had found.

I heard him say: "She helps everybody, and everybody likes her. She has never refused to do what I asked of her. Eve is my best n—."

This made my husband laugh. George could have said this in another way, but this was George Bone speaking. Despite his wording, it of course made me feel pretty darn good to know I was really appreciated.

However, I soon found out that George had another personality. When he had a snoot full of booze he became a madman. He would say nasty things to me and to others that were shocking. I was ready to quit this job so many times because I simply couldn't stand being belittled or being cussed at. Richard Rogerson would hold on to my hand and ask me to overlook a sick man's behavior.

"Poor George," Richard would say. "He really likes you, Eve. I know this to be a fact. But it is that damn booze that bewitches him and turns him against me, you, and, mostly, his wife. That is because we are closest to him and he feels like venting through us without any harm, or so he thinks. We are trying to get help for him because Ann is suffering badly. Please don't pay any attention to him and don't let him hurt you. You can do that, I know you can."

In the morning, or sometimes the next minute, George would forget he was mad at me and turn civil and sweet, and so I would forget his insults and I did not quit.

5 – Signs of Deep Friendship

The many signs of deep friendship between George Bone and Dick Poole were apparent. As early as my first week on the job I saw them playing pool early in the day, huddling and discussing important business matters. George won the game most of the time, although Dick Poole used to belong to the Professional Pool Players Society years back when he was still in the Coast Guard. Still, I could never figure that out because I used to be able to take George in a game of Eight Ball quite easily, and I was only a "Saturday night husband and wife player." My boss used to stride beside the edges of the pool table in his boustrophedon style, stopping to aim his cue stick and eye potential shots. George's hands shook badly, but he loved to win. He'd dance around in the hallway like a ballerina, hollering and bellowing, "Yay! Hey! I won, I won!" He wanted everyone in town to know he had won a game of pool.

I saw Mr. Poole pull out his own money from his pocket and pay the Coke deliveryman for that day's drop-off because George did not have enough cash on him. And I learned that when George paid him back, George would give Poole an extra twenty-dollar bill for his kind gesture. This happened many times over. Once, after witnessing such a delivery and payment by Mr. Poole, I commented to George, saying that he was a kind man. George was quick to say how kind Mr. Poole was, and told me that Poole spent every Saturday morning giving a crippled neighborhood man a bath.

"I don't know of another person who is as gracious as Dick Poole," George told me that morning. "His neighbor is an old guy and is partially disabled from a stroke. He belongs in a nursing home but they can't afford to pay a facility, so Mr. Poole helps the old woman out by giving her man a bath every week. I think that is something!" George concluded.

6 – The Morning of My Husband's Slipped Disc

Sometimes things happen that are so bizarre, it makes one believe supernatural help lurks near or in our own domiciles. Tuesday, November 12, 1975, is the date of my example of this.

My husband and I had relocated to Northeast Florida and were meticulous in our approach to our new positions here. I had been careful not to be late or absent from my new job on Bone's Pier where I was still a probationer under the watchful eye of Mr. Bone. Jobs were scarce during that period of national recession, and I had been mindful not to spoil my chances for earning extra money, as we had a new grandson and Christmas was coming fast.

On this day my husband awakened me at four o'clock in the morning with loud moans and outbursts of painful cries. It so happened that when he was getting up for a bathroom call, he was dropped prone by an old slipped disc problem. The disc had moved out of its place, was pressing on nerves, and he was wild-eyed and trembling with extreme pangs of pain, a scene I had seen many times before. When that disc slipped out of place, the poor man was usually thrown into a mental state close to insanity caused by the intensity of piercing stabs in his lower back.

"Please, call a doctor," he urgently instructed me.

I first ran downstairs to make a cold pack. This had been advised during an earlier episode. Luckily I found enough ice for a big fat pad. But Linwood insisted he was suffering excruciating pain and needed a doctor's help to quiet it.

"Please call a doctor!" he yelled again and again.

From past experiences I knew that after a doctor's office hours, we had to get to a hospital for medical treatment … and that motion was not something he could handle due to the fact that even the smallest movement caused unmerciful pain.

"I have to urinate, please hand me the urinal," he demanded.

I rushed to the closet and located this thing and rushed it back to him. But, as usual, my husband found it impossible to pass water while in a prostrate position, and he put the urinal aside. Now he suffered one stress on top of another.

The cold pack finally cooled his spine to where he was able to withstand the throbbing and he simmered down to a cold sweat. But now he was ailing elsewhere; his bladder was about to explode. He tried using the urinal again and again without results.

With the slightest movement, the condition of his back made him scream out as if a bloody murder was taking place in our house.

"Please call a doctor!" he begged.

I picked up the phone and dialed the number of Dr. Juan Aleman, the nearest doctor to our address, and let Linwood hear what I had just heard: "Our office hours are 8:00 a.m. to 5:00 p.m. If you have an emergency, please call the hospital."

"Do you want me to call an ambulance to get you to the hospital?" I asked.

"No, gosh darn it, no," he answered tearfully. "I cannot move. I cannot be tossed around like that."

It was now getting on towards seven in the morning, and I told him if he could hold out until eight o'clock, we would be more apt to find a doctor.

My husband had traced his slipped disc troubles back to World War II when he served in the US Naval Submarine Service, although this situation never got recorded on his health jacket. Linwood was a big man, six feet four and one half inches tall. On his submarine, the USS *Sablefish*, he slept on a bunk that he shared with canned peaches. Basically, he said, the bed was not long enough for him and the peaches. He slept with great difficulty until the stock was depleted.

He didn't have his first slipped disc problem until a couple of months after he was discharged from service; therefore we had trouble explaining to present-day doctors why this condition was not found on his medical records.

…

Linwood first experienced his slipped disc while he was in the middle of a sales presentation at Gimbels Department Store in Philadelphia, when he was employed by the Hamilton Watch Company. He said he no sooner had his sample trays pulled out to present the line, when he dropped to the floor as if he were shot in the back with a bullet. He said he couldn't move anything, he was so paralyzed with pain.

The buyer there called a doctor, who immediately gave Linwood an injection and sent him to Jefferson Hospital where he became the patient of a popular surgeon, Dr. F. Cappola. He began to prepare Linwood for surgery by draining his spinal fluid for analysis and asking if we had a blood donor for transfusions.

I had already signed an agreement for the surgery when I ran into Dr. Joe Brown, a brand-new physician from my old neighborhood. He asked what I was doing at Jefferson Hospital and after I told him how we got there and that my husband was about to enter surgery to have his disc removed from his spine, Joe became serious and warned me to back out of this procedure.

"I have the same damn problem," he said. "Because this operation to remove that certain disc is not yet perfected and can leave a man unable to bend enough to tie his shoelaces, I'm putting it off. Many tall men suffer with this same thing," he told me while holding my hand.

"The system will be perfected one day and until then I would not submit to this surgery if I were you. Tell your husband to lie on a firm surface until the disc slips back into its place, and he will be as good as new."

Much to Dr. Cappola's displeasure, I discontinued the surgery plan pronto, and we did what Dr. Joe Brown had suggested. The disc behaved after that for about a year, before it went out again. It usually happened in the fall or early winter. Dr. Judson, our New Jersey family doctor, gave him pain medication. Linwood would lie on the bare floor until the discomfort stopped, and he would be as good as new for another period. This happened numerous times over the years.

...

This morning Linwood's condition was distressful because he was so much in terrible pain, worse than ever before. This also put me into a dilemma because of my new job at the pier. This situation was making me ill; I was intent on keeping the job, and Mr. Bone expected me to come in to work at ten o'clock to help with the morning's surge of business. If I called in complaining of sickness, he might decide he didn't need me after all. But it did look as if I'd have to take the day off since I couldn't leave my poor darling man to suffer alone.

…

A loud noise in the front yard sent me running to see what had happened. An extension ladder leaned against the front of our townhouse, and I supposed that was what I had heard being placed there. A couple of young men were busily getting some things out of their van on the side street and I waited to see what they were up to. They soon came along with cans of stain and paint brushes, so I knew what they were about to do to the Martin Williams property. I recognized one of them as a young fellow I had met while fishing beside him on the pier.

"Hello there, Earl!"

Earl Voight was surprised to see me.

"Hi," he responded cheerfully. "So this is where you live. No wonder you're always on the pier. If I lived this close to it I'd be there every day too. This is my kid brother. We're going to throw a coat of Redwood Rez on your townhouse. How would you like that?" he joked.

It suddenly occurred to me to ask Earl for the name of a local doctor to call, and I told him what I had on my hands in the house. Earl immediately gave me the name of Dr. Doug Fowler, a known charismatic doctor who was also associated with a church on Atlantic Boulevard.

"This man is said to be a great doctor. He heals people charismatically, and I know that he makes house calls. He is the man you should have," Earl Voight concluded.

I suddenly got the impression that Earl knew this doctor quite well and I asked if he would please make the call to his office for me because I was a nervous wreck this morning. He readily agreed. I invited Earl into our townhouse and took him upstairs and introduced him to my husband, and explained to Linwood that Mr. Voight knew this special doctor and had agreed to make the call for us.

"And so we are as good as being on our way back to good health," I said, trying to sound in good spirits.

My husband, in a sweaty condition and badly needing to urinate, nodded in agreement. Then, almost in tears, he said, "I have to pee so badly I can taste it."

This sordid comment made Earl and me giggle.

Earl showed real compassion when he immediately said, "Don't you worry, Mr. Bates, Dr. Fowler will get you up in no time and you will relieve yourself of all that pressure. Don't you worry anymore, Mr. Bates."

Earl got the number from the operator, dialed, and the doctor answered. Young Voight nicely presented the situation in a few words. But I could tell by the strange look that suddenly came over Earl's face that things were not going as Earl had expected.

"Oh, I can't do that, Doctor, no sir, I can't do that, sir!"

Earl Voight's face and ears flushed a beet color. There was a long pause where the doctor was speaking and Earl was listening intently, and then we heard the click of the phone on the other end.

Earl turned towards me and my husband and said, "I have to do the laying on of hands because the doctor is scheduled to be at the hospital in fifteen minutes to operate, and he could not come here until this afternoon. He said that I must do it. He commanded me to do it. He gave me explicit directions. Please, Mrs. Bates, hand me your Bible."

I didn't know much about Bibles because we were a Catholic family, but I ran to the back room where we kept our books and brought Linwood's Bible. If I ever knew, I don't recall the passages he was instructed to use.

Earl was still red in the face when he found the page. With his trembling right hand on Linwood's forehead he proceeded in a strong quivering voice to read the passages. After he read what he was instructed to read, he told Linwood he was healed and could now get out of bed and go to the bathroom.

"Are you crazy, man?" Linwood protested vigorously. "Don't you understand, I cannot move a gol-darned muscle without agonizing, unbearable pain. I have a slipped disc condition!"

"Yes sir, Mr. Bates. You had a slipped disc condition!" Earl Voight nodded in agreement. "But now you don't have it. Please, Mr. Bates, try to get up and go to the bathroom. Come on, Mr. Bates, please try to get up to urinate. Here, hold my hand. I'll steady you while you turn your legs out of bed."

Lin decided to try what the young man said he must do, but I could see Linwood was prepared to fail. With wrinkled brow, gingerly, barely moving, he elevated his foot a fraction of an inch and discovered it somehow worked without pain. And so he began ever so slowly to lift his legs.

Like a snail, he turned himself sideways and shouted, "Holy smokes!" He lifted himself up into a sitting position. "I'll be doggone!" he puffed. "I feel no pain. You are a miracle man! What did you do to effect this?" he demanded of the young house painter.

"Mr. Bates, I'm just the instrument Dr. Fowler used. I only did what he instructed and demanded I do."

Linwood struggled awkwardly to stand, and with the young man's guiding hand he made it to a full stand-up position, towering above Earl Voight. He proceeded to put one foot in front of the other and slowly traipsed down the hallway to the bathroom, where he had needed to go for so long.

I looked at Earl who, I thought, was as astonished as we were. I cannot describe his countenance at that moment.

"I didn't know I could do this doctor thing," Earl whispered as he made his way out the door and back to his painting job.

I reported to work that morning and was even a bit early. Between 10:00 a.m. and the noon hour the pier business was brisk. Mr. Bone would have been annoyed if I had called in about a sickness that morning. As it turned out, when I made the story known, he told me I should leave at one o'clock if I wanted. Of course I was glad to be excused, and hurried home to keep my recuperating hubby company. I found him back in bed, fast asleep.

Remarkably, he never suffered from a slipped disc ever again!

Young Earl Voight was our guardian angel that day so near to Christmas. Oddly, I never saw or ran into that flounder fisherman ever again, even though I wound up working there for most of that decade.

We have often thought about this charismatic person and wondered how many other lives he had helped through the passing years. I have already stated that I believe fishermen and fisherwomen were the greatest class of people I had ever met, and Earl Voight is a classic example.

7 – Ann Bone

I was never formally introduced to Ann, Mrs. George Bone. I met her on my own after I was hired. I don't know why George didn't see fit to acquaint us, but I suppose he had his reasons, or he didn't know any better. They were not people who played holier than thou, I was certain of that.

...

Ann ran her gift store and rarely came to the tackle shop. She had a smart young woman clerking for her in the morning hours, and Ann usually came in after I was through with my shift, so we rarely found time to gab.

I used to see George visiting while sitting in the captain's chair beside Ann's stool, when I passed by her window on my way out to the pier. Her room, situated on the southwest corner of the pier building, had a very big display window on the mall side, and was the first thing one saw upon entering the facility. Her exhibiting window space was always attractive and eye-catching.

After I was hired, however, I don't remember seeing George sitting with Ann in her shop, or in the restaurant, or anywhere else for that matter. I soon learned that they were having marital problems and were about to separate. Richard Rogerson, one of their best friends, sadly revealed that Ann was really fed up with George's drinking and was ready to call it quits, being so unhappy with her life in daily turmoil.

A beautiful blond woman, Ann reminded me of the actress Ann Sothern: five foot six, eyes of blue-gray, with a satiny voice, and always with a soft smile on her pretty face. In her youth Ann had a knock-out body, but now that she was chasing fifty she showed definite signs of wear. Ann was afflicted with painfully crippling arthritis. Her stiffening legs and knees had slowed her walk, and her hands and fingers were terribly disfigured by this disabling disease. Yet, she was in love with her work and always looking for ways to improve her shop. She had her own car and was always on the go, chasing down stuff to sell. She knew all the local artists and crafting people.

Ann's retail store was not a typical seashore place loaded sky-high with all sizes and descriptions of T-shirts ready to fall apart in their first wash. She had a big department of T-shirts because they sold well, but her stock generally was of a fine grade, 100 percent cotton, and made in the United States of America. She once told me she wouldn't sell something she wouldn't buy herself. There was honest integrity behind her business. Her shop also revealed she had a taste for beauty and design. Even her huge collection of seashell artifacts was different from those in other local boardwalk stores, which came from China or Japan. In contrast, Ann sought out local artists and bought their finest work.

For instance there was Jessup Grant, a retired furniture designer down in St. Augustine, who collected local seashells. Grant turned these shells into the cleverest objects, such as mushrooms, toads, owls, and turtles. After Ann discovered him, she had trouble keeping Grant's artifacts in stock. But then, everything she bought resold well. She took time with her selections, choosing only what she considered a cut or two above the mediocre. Stylish bathing suits, footwear, eye shades, sun hats, jewelry, and colorful beachwear attracted customers. The walls in her shop were covered with handsome oil and water paintings by local artists, everything affordably priced.

I never heard George say anything disparaging about his wife during the whole time I was associated with the pier. They suffered in silence, as far as I could see. It got so we all knew George was sleeping on the cot in the back room at the pier's tackle shop, and Ann was going to the dog track with other people, such as Richard and Muriel Rogerson. George was drinking more and more heavily during 1974 and '75. He was getting himself in all kinds of trouble.

For instance, one day a young architect and his wife came to fish, and before the day was out—although George wasn't aware of it—George had commissioned him to draw up plans for an apartment to be built on top of the pier's roof. George showed the architect around on the roof and explained his desire for a private residence there. Looking for business, the hungry architect said he could oblige George with blueprints for a small modern apartment, and George said okay. They shook hands on it.

When the blueprints arrived by registered mail along with a bill charging three hundred dollars, George hit the countertop explosively, yelling, "I didn't charge the SOB for fishing. Why in hell is he charging me for these goddamn blueprints!"

George had no idea of the time the man had given to this project, and without looking at them he ripped up the architectural plans and heaved them into the wastebasket under the counter. This proved to me that he was never seriously considering moving out on Ann. All this came about because he had drunken pipe dreams. He went to court to resolve this unaffordable charge.

George's greatest problems were mostly concerned with the hired help. About this, he spoke to me often. He was always missing money. He called it "the leak" or "the goddamn leak." After he fired Bobby for stealing seventy-some dollars' worth of quarters, he hired an older man, thinking he had an honest face. This was Andy. Handy Andy, we called him.

Handy Andy was a pier worker with previous experience on one of the more southern piers. A dapper man wearing a well-trimmed mustache, Andy came to work in long sleeves and a necktie, wearing polished shoes, for crying out loud. He did look nice at the counter receiving customers, I must admit. The ladies always took a second peek at him. But Andy would not sweep, clean the toilet, or pack bait; he hired someone else to do these chores. However, he was absolutely professional and accounted for every cent he spent on the business of running the pier. If he paid one of the deliverymen out of the drawer, he placed a signed receipt under the cash drawer. Nevertheless, George felt he was still missing considerable amounts of money and appealed to me and Mr. Poole to help keep an eye on Andy and see if we could catch him pilfering in any way.

What type of a report Mr. Poole had given George is not known, but about the fifth or sixth month after Andy was on the job, Mr. Bone asked me if I could open the pier on Monday morning because he was firing Andy on Sunday night.

"I'm sick and tired of having this goddamn leak," he told me confidentially.

George didn't accuse Andy or tell him why he was letting him go; George had no proof for his reasoning. Andy, with a wife and two little boys to support, went to some labor board and complained he was discharged from a job without cause. George had to consult with a lawyer over that situation.

...

I never did understand why I was expected to work beside Dick Poole when I had already discussed my problem with his habit of cleaning out my cash drawer, for which I felt responsible. I remember how concerned Ann was about the amounts I thought were usually involved. When I told her that sometimes I knew I had taken in at least three to four hundred dollars for the half-day I was on duty, and when I counted up what I had after Mr. Poole left the pier, the drawer contained less than half that amount. Lately, I told her, this was happening daily, or every time he came up to the pier. I missed half of what I had taken in. That's why I approached Ann and asked who this man Poole was, because I thought that maybe he was a partner in the business and I should ignore what I thought was happening. Ann's eyes enlarged and she became alarmed.

"Oh my goodness, no! Poole is just a good friend who helps George out whenever he has the time. We wanted to hire him, but after Williams sold to us, Mr. Poole retired and didn't want to work steadily because he wanted to be free to be with his wife. But he kept coming to help out, and George slips him at least a twenty-dollar bill every day that he comes to participate for a couple of hours. He is well paid for what he does. He's been a big help to George. One of his duties is to watch the cash register and he has reported quite a few workers whom he claimed were taking too much for drinks and food. You know ..."

She stopped and was in deep thought for a moment. Then she said, "I've been wondering how the Pooles were able to trade their car in every year on a seaman's government pension. Maybe he has been helping himself here." She looked away, mulling it over.

Following that conversation I noticed that Poole was not invited to work unless George was there with him.

That day in particular, though, Poole was still hanging around while I was on duty, and I didn't like that one little bit. What George was doing, apparently, was keeping an eye on his friend more.

I later found out that George was quite angry at my disclosure to Ann about Poole. I had tried to discuss it with George, but goofy drunk, he had stopped me in my tracks. He simply did not want to believe Mr. Poole would take anything that did not belong to him. Although George thought for a while that I was wrong in going to Ann, in his foggy mind he did remember that I had tried to talk to him about Mr. Poole that day back when George complained to me that he had a big leak in his income. And I now know that he finally understood why I had to go to Ann with what was on my mind. I remember clearly how George had immediately declared to me that he completely trusted Mr. Poole so much so he forbade me to continue speaking further.

"I trust Mr. Poole completely. I would trust this man with my wife. He has done an awful lot around here and has never charged me a dime. Yes, I trust Dick Poole!" was the way George handled my attempt to discuss the situation with him that day.

I remember that George had been well pickled when I tried to get through to him. I felt desperate, so I had to try. But I was glad I took it up with Ann instead, and I know she understood why I had to go to her instead of insisting on dealing with pie-eyed George.

Still, a few weeks later, as far as I could see, Mr. Poole was still acting as my boss in George's absence, and this irked me terribly. I was ready to quit, but Ann, like Richard Rogerson, begged me to "Please ignore it."

They probably had a detective watching what was going on from one of the window tables in the restaurant. George never let me know that he'd had a deep conversation with Ann. He kept me in the dark about that despite the fact he was frequently telling me how he missed money from the business.

After my discussion with Ann, George was still drinking, but not as heavily as before. He was not clowning around in the hallway like he had been for a long time. He seemed to be more attentive to Ann and less argumentative with me and pier customers than before my talk with her. They were again sitting together in her shop, talking things over. They were attending the dog races together a lot more lately. Ann said the races were good for them both. They were able to sleep better when they hit the hay at the end of their day. Things were looking different after my talk with Ann, a bit calmer, I thought.

I don't know what was going on, but I learned about that same time that one night Ann thought George was having a heart attack and made him go see a doctor. He was instructed to slow down on the drinking and to come in for a complete physical examination.

8 – Ray Holt

Ray Holt was hired just ahead of me. I found this individual had a most annoying personality and if it weren't for Richard Rogerson's intervention I would have quit the pier mostly because of this individual.

At the dog track, George met and hired Holt to help unplug the main sewage line that led down from the pier and connected with the public sewage line on First Street. That day the three toilets in the restaurant and the one out on the pier against the east side of the tackle shop were backing up, and George needed to get this problem solved. Ray Holt claimed he did work like this, was willing to help, and was available immediately. George brought him home that evening.

They started at daybreak, according to fisherman Tiny Welsh, who witnessed those two working that early morning.

I hope that I accurately describe what Tiny said he saw happen. George Bone and Ray Holt were both wearing only swim trunks and using several lengths of connected garden hoses, when he came upon them shoving the hose up into the clogged refuse pipe from the clean-out plug down at the lower end of the pier. In this way they broke loose the jammed sewage line. Then suddenly, Tiny said, gravity took over and pulled the stinking blackish crap down the pipe with such force that it knocked them both off their footing and carried them and their big monkey wrenches a few feet in the sand and dumped them into the hole which they had dug to catch the sludge. Solid clumps of crap were everywhere, said Tiny.

The doused men struggled to recover their footing. The poop under the pier's entrance boardwalk, which missed the hole, quickly lost its stinking liquids into the beach sands. Bone and his hired man scraped up the solids and raked it all into a new hole Holt had dug. Both men were splattered from head to toe with putrid crap and waste matter, yet were having a riotous time laughing themselves silly.

"It was plain to see they both enjoyed the adventure, as well as the final swim to clean themselves up," Tiny said with a chuckle.

The weather was probably more at fault than the people. Nevertheless, I told Richard about a month into my employment that I was not able to take Holt and Poole, and especially not Ray Holt, a miserable-type person who constantly insisted on butting into my space. My diary's notation for April 4, 1975, states: *This new guy's personality is wacko. His way of life at the pier is to pick, pick, pick, and he thinks this makes him useful.* I resented him so much I was ready to quit. Richard kept pacifying me into putting up with everything "Just a little while longer." But it was not easy.

When spring's March, April, and May days rolled into Northeast Florida it was already steamy summer as far as I was concerned. I was trying to become accustomed to these local temperatures when it got into the nineties, and when June, July, and August arrived with those ninety-five and one-hundred-plus-degree temperatures, it was often unbearable to be outdoors in the midday humidity. That was when I got thrown in with these most difficult people I had ever met in my lifetime.

A top-grade alcoholic, Ray Holt wound up working daily for George Bone, and with boss-like privileges, which I couldn't understand. In the first place he had no idea of how to be in charge of anything, and I resented him telling me how to do things he knew nothing about.

At that early time of day there wasn't anyone else around for Holt to boss around except for me. Poole was the chief CEO and taught Holt how to open for business and what had to be done as a pier worker. Poole seemed to like Holt and they got along fine. So from mid-April, Holt opened the pier at 6.00 a.m., and by the time I came aboard at midmorning he was already drunk and argumentative as hell. It was plain he didn't want to leave the cash register, but he wasn't fast enough to take care of the growing line waiting to fish. I thought it was no wonder why Mr. Bone always missed monies, because he never looked into the background of anyone he hired. He didn't know a single thing about the Holts except that they knew how to pick a winning dog once in a while and they drank good moonshine, and that was all that seemed to impress George Bone.

Ray's wife, Tessy, was a ninety-eight-pound spook who could sit on her bony behind and stare into space all day long. A Mammy Yokum look-alike in a pantsuit, she was scary as hell with her large nose and bulging, watery and faded eyes. She always seemed to be unable to focus. George had asked her to watch over her husband more carefully and try to keep him sober while Ray was at work. She promised she would. But we onlookers could see she was a bona fide veteran alcoholic more interested in her own needs. Believing she was undetected, she sipped booze from a canister in her purse.

I have no time or respect for people like that. But Tessy never annoyed me or anyone else. Day after day, she sat alone in the corner of the restaurant, or on a chair or bench in the hallway until she fell over, and then Ray would pick her up and carry her down to their smelly little motorized trailer and let her sleep the day away.

"God Almighty," I used to say to Richard, "how wretched can some people become?"

If I were to say anything good about Ray Holt, I'd say he was a good worker—when he worked. Poole said he caught on fast to the routine. Ray even did more than was asked of him. He used to sweep the entire long pier with the wide push broom so that the previous night's peanut shells, shrimp skins, and other refuse were not annoying the new day's fishermen. Unlike me, Holt showed no interest in catching a fish, although he always enjoyed the fillets that I cooked up in the tackle shop's spider. He said he had no patience for the art of fishing.

Outside of George and Poole, he didn't make any new friends while at the pier. As a matter of fact, complaints began to appear. People approached Poole or me and expressed displeasure at the "rudeness of that new man." Then they described what he had said or done to displease them.

One mother of a perky twelve-year-old daughter took her indignation to Mrs. George Bone one day, where she explained Ray's unwanted comments, telling her kid she had "pretty virgin titties." Another time he laughingly told Mary Hart, one of the pier's lesbian fishing customers, that all she needed was "a good man to accommodate her sexually." And that is when Marion Moony, Mary's brawny companion, gave Ray Holt a hefty sock and blackened his eye.

Plenty of times, I felt like punching him in the gut for butting in with his incessant nasty comments. Mr. Bone finally decided he had better keep Ray Holt off the tackle shop counter due to Ray's "not being so good with the public." George tried to keep him busy working in the poolroom or some other place. However, Holt still thought he should hang around the register counter and drive me mad.

We usually had a sizable pile of newspapers under the front counter to wrap someone's fish or bait. One morning I was busily cutting up a big mullet for someone's bait on some of that newspaper when all of a sudden all hell broke loose.

"What the hell do you think you're doing here, Ms. Eve?" he exploded. "You are ruining our newspaper, and blah-blah-blah ..." He went on and on shamelessly, with completely nonsensical comments.

I couldn't stand it any longer! I picked up the whole thing, the mullet along with the bloody newspaper, and lobbed it straight into his head, as I yelled, "Get the heck out of here, Ray! Go find someone else to babble to, you crazy nutcase."

Now, George happened to be coming in and was close enough to hear what happened. He quickly led Ray away and put him to work elsewhere—and probably told him to lay off of me—because it was a little better after that day. God! What a sad-sack man that Ray Holt was.

He wasn't a bad-looking individual when sober, but he was never sober. He always came to work wearing shorts and sometimes a dirty T-shirt. He always wore flip-flops and mostly only a filthy pair of skimpy shorts. I guess he thought he was in vogue wearing scrawny beachwear on the pier. There was always a peculiar bad smell accompanying Ray Holt. I thought it was a heavy dose of B.O. Ray had told Dick Poole that he no longer had a working anal sphincter, having been ruined following surgery for hemorrhoids. According to Dick Poole to whom he confessed one day, Ray was unable to totally control his bowel movements. This was the reason, he said, why he was no longer employable. The man was only in his early fifties.

The reason he always wore flip-flops, he said, was because he was unable to get into a pair of shoes comfortably. I took a good look at his feet one day and was startled to see his right toe looked like a three-and-a-half-inch swollen penis with a foreskin covering a pink head.

The toenail was completely missing. The toe, he said, was a recent casualty; it was badly infected with a stubborn case of fungus.

Please, I thought, *stay away from me.*

ﻝ

9 – George Befriends the Wrong People

Harry Firestone, one of the regular fishing customers, began to hang out on the pier. He and his wife had recently separated because of his infidelities. She left with their three little girls and went back to her mother's home in Tennessee and filed for divorce. I happened to know other people who had children and divorced because of similar reasons, and I can't remember any single one who did not live in sadness and regret during and after the divorce, their hearts broken because of concern for their children. Harry showed no signs of remorse—not that I could see, he didn't. He soon lost his job at Lay's potato chip company and this gave him more time to fish by day and carouse at night.

Harry was a man who loved to brag about his escapades and conquests. It so happened that since George and his wife were separated, he now couldn't wait for Harry to come aboard to hear how he got laid the previous night by one delightful friend or another. George really admired Harry Firestone. Harry's way of life seemed to fascinate George. The two of them used to sit on the long bench in front of the restaurant and laugh belly-laughs at Harry's sexy tales and jokes.

When George found out that Harry had lost his job, he suggested Harry consider working on the pier. A position was open again. Harry was a strong, bulky man with a finely chiseled broad face and a loud, infectious laugh that tremendously appealed to George Bone. George needed a good, hefty man to help replace a half-dozen heavy pylons on the pier. He was happy when Harry agreed to work until something in his line of commercial electricity opened up. George not only found the brawny fellow he needed for the planned work ahead, he now considered Harry as a real true friend, and looked forward to having a pleasant relationship.

...

In the meantime it looked like Ann and George had made up again. It was noticed suddenly that he was drinking less and was again sitting in his captain's chair, happily having their private time together.

Richard Rogerson said they had better wake up and get their mortgage money together pretty soon, or Mr. Williams would be getting the pier back. Richard worried about his friends.

It seems the Bones were either spending too much money at the dog track or paying out too much to lawyers; they were having real troubles paying on their pier loan lately. I didn't know much about their private life, so this surprised me greatly. Richard, who also was a friend of the local dog track, said George and Ann liked to relax with the dogs at least three times a week in summer. And the way George was throwing his money around at the track it was no wonder he was having trouble managing financially.

"He is an absolute fool with his pocketbook," Richard said. "He'll put a ten-dollar bet on a sleeper and cry when the dog doesn't run to win."

"Oh, I guess I'd cry too," I said, laughing. "Does he drink at the track?" I asked.

"Do they still make booze?" Richard asked with a scornful smile. "Of course he drinks, and he pays for drinks for the gang that constantly hangs around him," Richard added. "There's a whole flock of people who stick around him like glue because they know he likes giving away those ten-dollar bills. He is quite popular at the track."

"So now he is up against it with his mortgage payments. That's sad," I murmured.

"The bets are on that he'll at least make it this month."

According to Williams, George shouldn't have to struggle like he was, at this time of the year.

"The pier has been doing good business. He's been spending too much foolishly," Richard sadly said. "George needs to sober up and find sober people to help manage the pier, or he will wake up and find himself reduced to bankruptcy."

"I know that Ray Holt is not much of a manager," I added in agreement with Richard's statement. "As a matter of fact, I think he is a drunken pain in the ass to customers as well as to most of us employees. To tell you the truth, Richard, this job would be enjoyable without Holt and Poole around to bug us. I don't know how much more I can stand of them," I confessed.

"If George were smart, he'd throw that pair into the ocean," Richard said, and laughed.

That was when I found out that Richard Rogerson had no time for either one of these two pier big shots. I felt a degree of comfort in knowing that our feelings were mutual here.

"George thinks he is getting the best deal with retired Poole because Poole is experienced and can take complete charge of things when George takes off for North Carolina," Richard knowingly explained. "George is after cheap labor. Neither of those two is on the regular payroll. George pays both of them by the day. He pays them well and thinks he's getting away cheaply, but he is losing more than he is saving with all that is happening of late under their guidance," lamented Richard Rogerson. Then he went on.

"At least we may become free from Holt pretty soon. I understand that Canadian authorities have already caught up with him and he is presently under probe. Holt may have to leave here and go home to answer to his government. Did you know that he is here working illegally?" Richard asked with a smile that betrayed his thoughts about Holt.

"No, I didn't!" I exclaimed in surprise. "I'm glad to say I'm happy with that bit of news. I can't stand much more of those peculiar Holts around me. God Almighty, that's good news to hear, Richard. Thanks for sharing this. When do you think this will happen?"

"Soon."

Now, I knew that Richard Rogerson, my friend and neighbor, was worrying the same as I had been about the way things were headed. Richard thought George was much too uncaring, the way he was gambling with Richard's part-time career at the pier. Richard wished not to have interruptions with his Slurpee business, at least not until he had enough money to pay his hospital bills and get his boys from his first marriage through college. This was first and foremost on Richard's mind.

For a while things looked good. One dark night, Tessy and Ray Holt disappeared from the pier, and we never saw them again.

George and Ann had made up. George seemed almost calm and less peevish or moody, and was noticeably drinking less. He and Ann seemed to have mended their differences and were buddies again. Richard and I were happily noticing the changes.

10 – Rogerson's Slurpee Story

Rogerson's Slurpee Stand was opened early in April when he saw the beach fill up on a hot day, and was shuttered up late in September when the place began to lose the sun worshipers. Virginia Snape, a retired lady who looked after the Rogersons' baby son, enjoyed opening the stand. She cleaned it daily, set it up nicely, and made Slurpees until a student, Otis, arrived after school. Otis came at two o'clock to take over the business for three or four hours, and then Richard arrived after his day at classes. The small stand was located halfway up on the north side of the boardwalk to the pier, so it was handy for thirsty folks to get a satisfying Slurpee fast.

When the restaurant was closed, business at Rogerson's Slurpee Stand increased greatly. People who went up to the pier with a beer or Coke in mind but found they couldn't get it, settled for a Slurpee. And they would buy three or four more for their folks down on the sand. Why not? Those Slurpees were amazingly wonderful … fruit-flavored, colorful, and refreshingly cold! Mm-mm, good. I loved the cherry-flavored icy cooler very much.

One morning, Virginia called in to say she was taken ill with a problem which prevented her from opening the stand. Ray Holt was still around then, and answered the call and told her not to worry. He managed to pick the lock and opened the Slurpee stand for business. George and Poole were not there to suggest or ask Holt to do that, but later Poole said he thought Holt was a good guy for trying to help out.

Holt said he used fifteen dollars of his own money for the opening bank, but after paying this back Richard Rogerson counted little more than that in the cash drawer. Something was plainly wrong. Richard saw that immediately. A busy day with little money to show for it is quite disappointing.

"No more! No more help from anyone, thank you!" yelled Richard, who found a lot of slop and wasted stuff on the deck and on the stand, and no money to account for any business done that day.

11 – George Celebrates His Birthday

On Tuesday, April 29, 1975, at one o'clock Ann threw a birthday party for George's fifty-fifth. She had a big tray of various cold cuts, a tray of all kinds of cheeses, and a huge rectangular chocolate layer cake. The goodies came from Publix, to commemorate his special day. So George and Ann Bone, Richard and Muriel Rogerson, Dick and Ida Poole, Harry Firestone, Ed and Gail Davis, and I all had lunch together on the pier … and we sang "Happy birthday, dear George."

Then Ann asked me to go out on the pier and invite all the regular fishermen and women to come have a piece of cake, and they, too, wished him a happy day, some kissed him, and others shook his hand. It was indeed good to see this man in a cheerful mood.

12 – Harry Firestone Now in George's Life

Harry Firestone was now keeping steady company with Adella Kripson. She had left her husband and was head over heels in love with Harry. She had two children, Kevin, ten, and Adella, a twelve-year-old who had back surgery as a baby and now was destined to wear leg braces for the rest of her life. Mother Adella must have had a miserable life until she met Harry, but we old-fashioned onlookers thought she was leaving the frying pan and jumping straight into open fire when we saw what was happening to this family.

A big, good-looking woman weighing almost as much as Harry, Adella had large, well-sculpted breasts. She was openly demonstrative with her affections for the new boyfriend. It was a guaranteed "fish and tit show," employee Scot Wood said with a laugh, whenever these two were on the pier fishing. Harry was a natural-born fisherman and knew how to hook a flounder as well as a Spanish mackerel. He taught Adella the art of catching fish so that he could take her out in his Cobia boat. Adella became as good at fishing as he. When the fish were not biting, Adella moved in on Harry and rubbed and massaged his back and sometimes his front, too. Then they absented themselves from the pier for an hour or so. It was no secret that she was a hot one, and Harry loved it that way.

In June, Ann Bone had to go to North Carolina for a week of family business. Harry lost no time convincing George to go out with them to have a good time. Since George had already been thinking that way for a while, he was easily convinced. Harry found Charlotte for George's companion and off the four went. George was already two sheets to the wind when they started. He thought he had to be a fool not to imbibe a few drinks while he had the chance. It did not take long before they wound up in a motel.

According to the way Harry told this sordid tale, it was a total disaster and it was all George's fault.

Harry said, "George had no idea how to behave. He did not participate in conversation of any kind. He never said a nice thing to his girl, and kept telling her she should go home because she was no good as far as he was concerned. Then he took a ten-dollar bill out of his pocket and threw it at her and said, 'Call yourself a taxi,' rolled over, and promptly went to sleep!"

Harry was really disappointed in the way their night had turned out. He'd expected to see that George Bone got screwed, blewed, and tattooed, all of which Harry thought George needed.

It wasn't long before Ann found out about this tryst, and Harry Firestone got fired, but not by George.

Ann faced Harry in the hall in front of her shop and said in no uncertain words, "Out! Get out of here. I never want to see you around here ever again!"

George looked at Harry and shrugged his shoulders, indicating: *What can I say, Harry? Ann is the boss around here!*

According to Harry Firestone, he thought George had made a confession to Ann that George thought would do him some good. And it probably did.

13 – Ralph Haack

It was a change of pace when our good friend Ralph Haack arrived from Warrenville, Illinois, with part of his baseball team. They were on their way to the Cayman Islands for their annual scuba diving outing. They planned to spend three days with us first. Our young guests were Lanny Haack, Johnnie Sabarbrow, Tommy McNellis, and Jimmy Lederman, all in their mid-teens. They arrived late at night on April 11, and of course they slept in for an hour or two before they came to the pier to fish. They paid their way in with George (who didn't know they were my houseguests until after I came in from the pier and excitedly told him about my visitors). And when the boys found me sweeping grimy parts of the pier, they took over and swept it all the way from east to west, and showed George their best.

Then they commenced to catch whiting and all kinds of fish with their light freshwater gear. It was a good fishing day. About that time George had me do some fishing every morning and he would scale and clean whatever I caught and freeze the fillets for his brother Leaston, back home in North Carolina. That day Ralph and his gang caught at least fifty pounds of fish, which they scaled and dressed before presenting it to George. Naturally, George gave them a free pass, and they caught another mess of whiting for him the next day. Ralph said that the boys talked about "catching fish on Eve's pier" long after they got back home.

That last night we all dined on trout almandine made from fillets of freshly caught bluefish, but named after a more noble ocean specimen. Mr. Ralph Haack, the first-class amateur chef of Warrenville, Illinois, prepared, seasoned, and cooked our magnificent dinner. And they didn't let me wash a single dish. This is what I call "spectacular company"! I was saddened to see them depart.

14 – Poole Leaves with a Policeman

A Jacksonville Beach policeman came to the pier one Saturday noontime looking for Dick Poole.

Mr. Poole's Adam's apple flopped up and down as he swallowed, saying, "Yes, sir. What can I do for you?"

The policeman did not isolate Poole. He came right out with his business, softly saying, "Mrs. Jones sent me to ask if you know what happened to her husband's two-carat diamond ring." The cop stared into Mr. Poole's watery eyes and waited for an answer.

Calmly, Mr. Poole said, "How should I know? He loses it all the time. But he was wearing it this morning when I gave him his bath."

"That seems to be the trouble," the policeman said. "Mrs. Jones is certain he had it on this morning, but it was missing after you left their place. She called us thinking you might have taken it." Again he looked at Mr. Poole's face like a professor studies a problem.

"What would I want with that old man's jewelry?" Mr. Poole asked, but quickly said, "He loses that ring all the time. It is probably down in the folds of his easy chair."

"We searched the room thoroughly, but it wasn't found," the cop argued.

"Well, I don't have it," retorted Poole. "I'll bet you I will find it. Let's go take a look around," he offered.

The cop motioned to the doorway, willing to give Mr. Poole his chance.

A half hour later Dick Poole was back on the pier, so we knew he had not been arrested for stealing Mr. Jones' diamond ring. He was, however, boiling mad to the core.

"Today was the last bath I'll ever give that crazy SOB," Mr. Poole explained to George Bone.

His comment was heard by a dozen or more people.

"You and everybody else here saw how dangerous it is to fool around with nuts like old man Jones, who no longer knows the time of day. I stuck my hand down into the side of his Stratolounger chair, and there it was. Apparently, after his bath his finger had shrunken enough so that his ring actually fell off and rolled down unseen. But I didn't appreciate the fact they thought I had taken it! The bastards!"

George poured a couple of water glasses half filled with Ancient Age bourbon whiskey and together with his good buddy, Dick Poole, drank to the health of Mr. and Mrs. Jones, "Those SOBs."

15 – Break-Ins

The things that used to upset George to no end were the break-ins and petty thieveries. The pier was broken into numerous times. It happened twice on my watch. The first time, according to my notes, it happened on May 9, 1975, on a Friday night. George Bone was as nervous as a cat on hot cinders when I arrived at eight in the morning. It so happened that George opened that day, and it was he who found the place had been broken into, ransacked, and stuff had been taken. This was the same day that George and Ann Bone had to go to court to be charged by Ms. Johnnie Hexton, and George was already upset over that. Now this!

When I arrived, I found him shouting and cussing like a mule skinner.

"Goddamn it to hell, never a dull moment around here," he whined.

At low tide, when cars could be driven under the pier, the thief gained access by climbing the pier's pylon up to the porch of the restaurant. He broke the window on the restaurant's porch and then walked in and all about the pier-house, choosing stuff he would carry off. "He must have been a goddamn roughneck kid," George said, "because the thief only found and took the opening cash in the gift shop." George also found that the new, large, expensive Shakespeare rod-and-reel combo was taken from the tackle shop, and a bunch of beef jerky and candies were missing from the restaurant. George said the insurance company rarely covered what was taken, and decided not to even call them on this particular robbery.

On May 14 my notes tell me that: *Ed Davis went out to the end of the pier this morning with his .38 pistol to check out the mysterious guy spotted out there before the pier was open for business. He found it was one of the shark fishermen from Welaka, Florida, who had secured permission from George to stay over. George forgot to pass on the information.*

The second time I was privy to a break-in was on Thursday, November 27, when I opened at seven in the morning and discovered what had happened during the night. Actually I discovered this along with Tiny West, one of the regular morning fishermen. Three-hundred-pound Tiny was waiting for me at the door, which he said was already ajar. So he was the first to know that the pier-house had been entered illegally. Together we went into the building. Thank goodness Tiny was there, for I remember being scared breathless. I was afraid someone was still in there and was about to clobber us over the head with a pool stick. No one was inside the building.

Together, Tiny and I found how they had entered. A windowpane had been broken out from the outside on the rear hall door next to the tackle shop. This meant they had climbed the pylons up to the pier's deck at low tide.

This yegg must have had an accomplice to hand stuff down to; a half dozen brand-new rods and reels were gone, several fresh boxes of Sea Hawks, and all of the new knives had been taken from the tackle shop's display case. I noticed my personal Shakespeare rod and reel also missing from a peg on the back wall. So was George's private gear. They didn't find the pier's hidden opening bank; however, they had cleaned out the little bank in the gift shop.

A second early-morning fisherman entered and when he discovered what had happened, told us he had been sitting in his car in the parking lot and saw a guy at five o'clock in the morning coming down from the pier's ramp, who had hopped off and headed north on the beach. He was carrying nothing that could be seen. This fisherman described the man as a "tall young man between twenty and twenty-five years of age, with fine features and brownish messy hair." This witness described details that fit about a hundred or more fellows who fished this pier. This guy also said he asked this person what time the pier opened, and was told, "At six or seven o'clock." George estimated he had lost a few hundred dollars again.

My notebooks don't indicate whether George reported this robbery to his insurance company, but I was aware that he was in touch with them more often than he cared to be.

16 – Bobby Stacker

In the middle of April, I witnessed another dastardly happening. George fired Robert (Bobby) Stacker this day. Bobby was a good-looking free-lance electrician from North Carolina whom George hired to wire the intercom to the very end of the pier. When I began to work there the system was newly installed, and I found it saved a lot of steps for us workers.

Now George wanted Bobby to wire some walls inside the pier with indirect lighting. Bobby showed up around 9:30 a.m. and said he "Couldn't work that day due to some important business with his insurance company, in order to get his driver's license back."

He figured this amount of reasoning would satisfy the boss. However, he was in for a surprise.

This line infuriated George Bone and he yelled out, "You're fired! You lying son of a bitch! You already have your license. You got it back yesterday. What are you trying to pull off around here?" George didn't say how he found this out, but he was plenty mad! "Here is twelve bucks for the hour or so you have done here."

George counted the money out, laid it on the counter and, without looking back, walked off to some other interest in the poolroom.

Bobby regarded me strangely, like with a half-smiling and half-crying expression, then picked up the money. I could see he had something important on his mind.

"I wanted to borrow a hundred bucks from George," he said slowly and sadly, "but I suppose that's not possible now."

I shrugged in response, to indicate it wasn't any of my business what he had in mind. Bobby looked at me pitifully, as if I were supposed to know he had great troubles.

About then his girlfriend joined us, and they went into the restaurant for breakfast. His significant other was seven months pregnant, at merely seventeen years of age. A runaway, she had come down to Florida with a girlfriend from South Carolina, but after she met Bobby she decided to stay with him when her friend returned home. Bobby was ten years older than her. They cohabited in a small one-room apartment right from the start of their friendship. They adopted a little dog to keep her company while he worked around. They seemed to radiate happiness whenever I saw them together.

Then the real shocker hit. At precisely eleven o'clock that day, a well-dressed woman and two little handsome kids arrived in the pier's hallway. This happened to be Bobby's legitimate wife and his two boys, about three and four years of age. They had driven from Georgia to reclaim their husband and father.

Although Bobby knew they were coming to take him back home, he didn't explain anything to his girlfriend. Bobby rushed out of the restaurant and swooped over his kids. Hungrily, he picked up first the younger one and then the bigger one, turned his wife around, and rushed them down off the pier and out of our sight.

The pregnant girlfriend came out of the restaurant and sat down on the long bench in the hallway and began to weep. I took a cold Pepsi to her and asked where she grew up. I told her she must now go straight home to her mother, and she nodded in agreement.

According to the girlfriend, "Until this very last minute," Bobby had never told her he was married and had children. She had no money. Bobby didn't even think to give her part of the money received from George that morning.

George Bone, however, provided this poor, unfortunate girl with twenty-five dollars, enough for some lunch and fare to get on a bus to her South Carolina home. His heart was like that.

Richard Rogerson said there were many runaways that sooner or later would show up at the pier begging for something to eat. "The woods are full of them down here," he told me. Within a year's time I found this to be absolutely true. There were many runaway kids in Florida.

I have often wondered how this young mother-to-be fared in her lifetime.

17 – Johnnie Hexton's Restaurant

George was going nuts concerning problems with his restaurant and Ms. Johnnie Hexton. His difficulties began a couple of years before, when he first allowed Johnnie to rent there. She was not the type for this fishing pier. It started simply. She would not open early enough for his clientele; but his real big troubles with her began in April, after he wrote and told her to find herself another place; he wanted his restaurant back. That was after she skipped days at a time of remaining closed. Usually the reports were that she was holed up in her beach cottage, coming down from a drunk.

George became enraged and difficult to live with. Because of him, I was ready to throw in my towel; I didn't need all this negative drama.

My records dated Wednesday, April 9, 1975, state: *I don't think I care to keep working on the pier because of all the heavy drinking, especially by George. I cannot make heads or tail from his conversations anymore. His angry, nasty, perplexed, and confused personality is more than I care to contend with. I think Richard Rogerson will understand my position. I thought working on the pier would be like a Shangri-la for me, peaceful and idyllic, but here instead, I get loaded down with so many ugly problems of late. I don't need this craziness in my life.*

On this particular April day I saw, for the very first time, George drinking vodka straight from the bottle at nine o'clock in the morning. I had hoped he cared enough for Ann to curb this habit of getting drunk, at least enough to save his marriage.

This month when Johnnie Hexton actually got a written notice that they were kicked out as of the 23rd of the month, things went from bad to worse. Johnnie refused to move out. She seemed to want to continue doing business sporadically. When she was around, George was a wild man, angry all day long. That meant we all had to put up with his wearisome nastiness, and it lasted from mid-April until the last of June.

During this time George's drinking progressed even more, if that were possible. He was never sober that I could see. He was now buying three quarts of AA 20 Years Whiskey every day. Either Dick Poole or George would send me out to make the purchase. George offered drinks to friends who stopped by. Dick Poole did his share of the daily drinking, but he could restrain his capacity better than did George. I never saw Dick Poole bleary-eyed drunk. He'd get silly and laugh at things that I didn't think funny, like at George, for instance.

It was my idea that I was looking upon tragedy when George went nuts. For instance, this man was not only facing losing his wife, but also his real estate because of his inability to focus on realities.

Ann Bone, about this time, told me that, yes, a divorce was imminent; she couldn't stand George any longer. She admitted she was talking to a lawyer. She said their big beach house was for sale since they had to scale down and use the equity to satisfy their present mortgage payment. George kept up his early-day drinking as if he was unconcerned about those things.

In fact, he was getting so loop-headed and out of control with his actions that in the morning hours after breakfast, he would put on an artsy show for everyone in the hallway. He played tunes on someone's lost ukulele (which he did not know how to play); he crooned Bing Crosby–style to an embarrassed captive listener; he whistled like a bird for another party caught in the hallway on his way out to fish. Nobody knew what to say or do regarding him and his nerdy performances. They looked at me with the most quizzical expression on their face, wondering what was wrong with the man. It was serious. It was awful.

Johnnie thought she had a legal leg to stand on, so she consulted with a lawyer and refused to move out. Her lawyer thought he understood she was complaining of being taunted unnecessarily and wrote George advising him to come to court to answer Johnnie's charges.

George had already committed the restaurant to Mr. Ed Davis to be the next manager and tried not to pay too much attention to Johnnie and her threats. But she was an item when she wanted to be. Loud and coarse, she opened the restaurant, only it was every other day, selling cold soda and hot coffee, but she was without a crew and the means to cook food. Florida Power and Light had shut off the electricity for nonpayment of service.

To avoid complications with the lawsuit, George refrained from entering the restaurant. However, one early morning Dick Poole went in and inspected the kitchen equipment. He reported to George exactly what was happening with stuff in the freezers and cold locker rooms. Ann Bone called the Board of Health and asked them to come take a look. They officially closed the restaurant for four days, not to be opened before they inspected again.

George sent young Daryl, Joey, and Smitty into the kitchen to thoroughly clean out the freezers, refrigerator, and cooling room. Those boys sweated over this smelly job. They threw out the spoiled stuff and washed everything down with hot soapy water. Proud of their work, they were now sitting on the long bench in the hallway cooling off when Johnny came roaring into the building and restaurant.

When she saw what had happened, she stood the hall and screamed at the boys, "Who was in my locked restaurant? Was George in here? This place was locked!"

"No, Miss Johnnie, this door was not locked," protested Joey.

He got up and went to the second door and freely swung it open to show her what he meant. With that, Johnnie threw a fist at Joey, who raised his arm and deflected the force.

Ann Bone was in her shop and saw Johnnie heave that fist at the kid. She called the police. They came and marched Johnnie off the pier.

George and Ann went to court on Thursday, June 12; I had to work alone that day from four o'clock until closing as a result. The case was rescheduled and they had to appear in court one more time. George got his restaurant back on the 30th of June. I was happy, of course, because George was happy and was behaving decently towards everyone that day. It was like a celebration: Hurray, hurray, Johnnie has finally gone away!

18 – Ed Davis Opens the Restaurant

In comparison, Ed Davis and his wife were a quiet couple as they worked feverishly to move in to do business. Gail, his third wife, was at least fifteen years younger than Ed. Shapely and slim as a reed, she was a sparkling, good-looking brunette.

A tall, thin-framed man, Ed Davis was a double for famed Hollywood personality Clint Eastwood. He even carried the quiet persuasiveness about him as did Mr. Eastwood.

I witnessed George's first flare-up at Ed Davis. George found out that Ed was still without a beer license.

He yelled at Davis, "I don't see how you expect to run a successful restaurant business without a beer license. I thought you told me it was in the works."

Ed Davis, like his honorable look-alike, stood tall before George Bone and with a straight face and a twinkle in his eye, he said, "Mr. Bone, don't you worry, it's still in the works."

As it turned out, his wife's mother arrived from Chicago, and the Florida liquor license was obtained in her name.

"Why is that?" I asked with curiosity and some surprise.

"Ed Davis can't legally apply for a liquor license," George answered rather harshly.

"Why?" I said in a softer voice.

"Because he is an ex-convict, he has served time, that's why." George drooped his head sadly.

"What'd he do?"

"He was convicted for bootlegging, that's what."

Boy-oh-boy! George, you certainly know how to pick your businesspeople! I was thinking.

Ed Davis was a hardworking man, that much I knew for certain. It only took him and his crew three days and three nights to set up shop and they opened to a flood of business. We all wished the Davises much success.

Not only a promising businessman, Ed Davis was also locally well known as a devout fisherman. During the first week of his grand opening of the restaurant, he masterfully showed quite a large crowd of people on the pier how to bag a big tarpon. Not that he wanted it for his restaurant—it was not useable as food—it was for show. The pogies, or menhaden, were running close to shore. Ed knew that come high tide that evening, the tarpon would herd them even closer to shore before they attacked and started a feeding frenzy in shallower water.

People saw two men in a small boat coming from the north. They didn't know that it was Ed Davis with a comrade who was slowly driving Ed's special skiff, equipped with a special motor, which he used mostly in the Intracoastal Waterway. On this day, the ocean was like a calm lake and this open boat was just right. Fishermen on the pier could see the pogies blipping and jumping up out of the water as huge fish showed their broad backs and tails while they rolled and turned on top of the menhaden.

The menhaden school was drifting towards the south, and now the skiff was drifting with the school, surrounding it. When they were the right distance away, in front of the pier, Ed stood up in his boat and began to cast his bait, a live pogie pinned through its back and tail with a couple of number three circle hooks, on a five-foot-long, sixty-pound test monofilament leader. He threw the bait out over the school one time, and *pow*! He had his tarpon hooked. That tarpon skyrocketed out of the water three times right in front of the pier's crowd, and each time, we saw Ed bow to his leaping fish to keep it from snapping a taut line. Finally, the monster turned and headed north, pulling the boat behind. By now everyone saw it was Ed Davis who was showing off for them. Davis fought that giant tarpon for a good half hour and wound up about a half mile north of the pier before he brought it to his skiff and released it for another day's fun. Tarpon are not a species used for human food anyway. They are used only for sport fishing.

19 – Pier People

As the ocean gets warmer each day after the spring equinox, more fish appear. Through the winter months and up to about the middle of February, we don't see many flounder, Florida pompano, ocean trout, or other weak fish until the waters heat up to sixty degrees. And when it gets warmer, these staple varieties are sought after vigorously.

By the end of May every variety is moving northward in a mass migration within the sloughs of the surf. By then the pier becomes loaded with fishing people. Fathers and grandfathers with sons and grandsons are seen daily as they cast for blues or whiting. Many women have taken up the hobby of fishing, often on a daily basis.

Sometimes the monofilament lines of six or seven people become entangled so badly that an expert has to cut them all apart and retie them from scratch. That was part of my job. Everyone who worked on the pier had to know how to handle these intertwined snarls. Some people thanked me for this help, while some cussed at me and others because it happened.

Often these snags occurred because "green" fishermen threw their lines helter-skelter, crossing over all their near, and sometimes far, neighbors' lines. When George was sober he used to be an expert at this; he'd get them apart with some humor. But when he was drinking he was much too caustic with people's feelings. He'd bawl out the person whose line he found had caused the damage, and sometimes there would be an argument over who was really to blame.

Generally speaking, some folks have yet to learn good fishing etiquette. It is so important when fishing near another person who might be seriously trying to catch a fish for supper, not to interfere in his space. That is why throwing the line straight out at a forty-five-degree angle to the pier's edge is important. If all the fishermen practiced good fishing manners, there would be no terrifying muddles to fuss over.

Speaking of "terrifying," we sometimes actually encountered people on the pier who had thalassophobia, the fear of the sea. When their anxiety had turned to panic, they asked us for help. We gave them a glass of water or soda and suggested they go home to rest.

On the pier, the matter of noisemaking and loud music is also frowned upon by serious fishermen. And they will kill your dog for sniffing around their bait bucket. No fisher person worth his salt will allow dogs, or pets of any kind, to touch their fish enticements or bait bucket because they know that the denizens of the deep have a keen sense of smell and might refrain from taking that lure. It's the same reason true fisher folk will not fish until washing their hands after touching gasoline-using equipment. Mr. Williams was such a man, so he had a rule disallowing dogs on the pier. And George, a serious fisherman, had the sign repainted and rehung in agreement to this.

One Saturday morning early in May, I was working in the pier's parking lot chasing out surfers and beach people, pleasantly explaining that the pier's private parking space was only for fishing people. We expected a big crowd. "Sorry, boys, it's the boss' orders," I explained.

That was when I first heard a couple arguing. They had their fishing gear out of their camper and were ready to go aboard the pier. Plainly, their dispute was over their dog. It sounded like an important quarrel.

The girl screamed, "F— you, Johnny!" in finality, and with a blanket over her arm she and her doggie hurried away from him and their rig, and climbed up on the boulders beside the pier where she found a flat sitting spot. This was at ten o'clock in the a.m.

The parking lot was now full, so I went back to the tackle shop to help George at the register. People found places to park their car on side streets now, and kept coming aboard to fish. Pretty soon one of these oncoming people told me there was an accident down on the rocks and a lady was bleeding and screaming for help. I called George back from the poolroom to cover for me and went to see what that report was all about. People were always reporting things at the tackle shop desk, and it was our job to check things out.

I found the girl who had run off from her man, now bleeding from a nasty knee bruise caused from a fall she had on the granite rocks. I helped get her off that huge perch and up to the hallway on the pier, where I gave her first aid with peroxide and some huge Band-Aids. She was inconsolable, and seemed to be on something, I wasn't sure what. I didn't smell booze on her person, but then I'm told there is stuff that you can't smell.

She was a pretty girl, in her late twenties. I thought she resembled Nancy Sinatra Jr.

I asked for her husband's name and called him on the intercom, saying, "Johnny, please come to the tackle shop, Joanie needs to see you."

When her strikingly good-looking hubby arrived, I heard an amount of squeaking and crying, along with a terribly loving apology on both their parts and I could see that all was forgiven. He took her out to the middle of the pier, where they settled down to do some fishing.

George went home around eleven. He and Ann were planning on a matinee trip to the dog races that afternoon. Ann called at twelve o'clock to ask if someone was there to relieve me, and of course Dick Poole was dutifully waiting to be of help.

At one o'clock my time was up, but before leaving for home I went out to the end of the pier to see what the "real" fishermen were catching. All was quiet out there. They said there was a state of high tide dullness for about an hour, and several couples were taking a nap while holding onto their reels. I wished Mike Chakos and Doug Johnson good luck for the day.

On my way back I saw someone jump down into the water at about midships. I ran up and leaned over to see what was going on there, and immediately recognized the man in the water as Joan's husband, and he was in real trouble!

"Call 911! Somebody please call 911!" I yelled to the people crowding around me. "Call 911, and please hurry, this man is in trouble!"

Mr. Johnny wasn't swimming! Not even a little bit. Either he didn't know how or he was just plain tired out from the jump down. The water was deep there, about ten or twelve feet. He was drifting away from the pier with his arms hanging out loosely and not moving. His face was now below the water line, his unfocused eyes open, and his body was sinking down.

Wow! I thought. *This guy is drowning as I watch!*

I turned towards the end of the pier where they had ropes, and with my tongue curled against my teeth I gave a couple shrill whistles for attention, adding a hand-over-hand signal for a rope. The boys out there knew what I meant!

Out of the crowd that was growing larger beside me, Young Red leaped over the rail, down into the water, and grabbed hold of the sinking Mr. Johnny. Young Red had been heading for the tackle shop for a swivel when he looked over the edge and saw the man going down again. Red was merely a slip of a teenager alongside the other. But this kid knew what to do. Young Red dove down and came up behind Mr. Johnny.

However, he could do little else, and he cried out, "Help! Help!"

A couple of sailors from the end ran up with some rope. One jumped overboard while the other threw down the line. The sailor in the water wrapped the rope around the drowning man's mid-body and the other sailor pulled him up out of the water enough so he could breathe air. Mr. Johnny hung there, showing no signs of life.

Now the problem of pulling Mr. Johnny up was next. The pier's deck stood at least twelve feet above the water. No problem here! Several shark fishermen jumped on the line and, in a flash, hauled Mr. Johnny up and he was now lying on the pier's deck. He was not moving and not breathing, though. One of the sailors swiftly turned him over and, kneeling over his body, pushed down on his back and shoulders, and we saw a bunch of water emit from Mr. Johnny's mouth.

Then we heard the rescue wagon wailing its way nearer. Still the man was not breathing, and the sailor kept using the old-fashioned back-pressing action. Finally, we detected a squeak of a sound and a small movement of his arm—not much—but convincing us the effort must go on. In no time at all the gurney rolled up and the professionals picked up Mr. Johnny. All others were pushed aside. The medics began administering oxygen and stuff they had to do as they swiftly wheeled him off the pier, to their ambulance parked inside of the pier building's large double doors.

Along with her unconscious husband, the weeping Joanie was packed off to the Beaches Hospital about two miles away.

Phew! Gosh! What excitement for everybody on the pier that day! The people who were fishing neighbors of this couple identified them as Johnny and Joanie Evanich, who had a bar business in High Springs. They had been arguing about their dog all day long, they said. She insisted on bringing her darling cocker spaniel out on the pier under cover, beneath a blanket, despite the fact that her husband begged her not to. The people said she had the dog hidden, but the animal was hot and cried out unmercifully. The nearby fishermen said they were annoyed by the crying dog and by the loud hard-rock music the couple played. The onlookers didn't know what it was, but they said he jumped into the ocean to recover a packet of pills which accidentally slipped out of Joanie's hands and popped over the edge and out of sight. It was established: Johnny had jumped into the ocean to retrieve her pills.

Later that evening I drove over to the hospital to see how the drowning victim had made out. I found the handsome Mr. Johnny sitting on the side of his bed, and his room was filled with visitors. He was smiling brightly and thanked me for coming by.

For me, this made the end of that day just perfect.

20 – Workers of Italian Descent

George once told me that he had never met a person of Italian descent while growing up in rural North Carolina. But after he had seen several films about these people, in *The Godfather* series, he had decided they were worth befriending. He actually believed they knew how to make money and have law and order in life.

That was why he decided he'd like to hire Dominick d'Aleo to open and manage the pier. Dominick was exactly the same size and age as George, with a totally gray head, which appealed to George to have at the register. Dominick was a good-looking, first-generation Italian American, and he had impeccable manners.

Dominick and Rose d'Aleo had retired from their Brooklyn shoe repair shop after thirty years and moved to Jacksonville, Florida, to be close to their daughter who was an art teacher at the nearby St. Johns River Community College. Dominick was a no-nonsense fisherman and was not only astonished, but also delighted, when George asked if he'd ever consider working again.

"Yes, I am thinking about it. Are you offering me a job?" asked the sober-faced Dominick one morning when both happened to be at the coffee maker.

"When can you start?" the surprised pier owner asked.

"Right now. What do you want done?"

George Bone admired people who were able to act spontaneously. He explained the opening procedures and told Dominick that his old-time best friend, Dick Poole, would be around to assist and answer any and all questions in George's absence.

A frequent visitor to the pier, Dominick already knew most of the regulars and probably also had a good idea of what the job entailed. Dominick agreed to work Monday through Friday and once in a while he'd work a half day on Saturday. He made it clear from the start, however, that he would not miss Holy Mass on Sundays, no matter what situation was at hand. He and George Bone had a good understanding from day one.

Dominick and I had already known each other and he knew I had been hired to help at the tackle shop through the busiest business hours. We were friends from the earliest hour. What a difference it was to work with a sane person, I told Richard Rogerson, who also liked Dominick d'Aleo.

...

When Carmelo Ausli saw Dominick on the job, he too decided to ask for work on the pier. Mr. Bone hired Ausli for the closing position. George was happy with his selections, especially when he found out that Ausli was handy with a gun. George figured there would be fewer break-ins with Ausli around.

Laura and Carmelo Ausli had retired from a small neighborhood grocery store business in the Italian section of Brooklyn, New York. They sold out and took their first trip to Florida. After spending a year living in different areas they decided that Northeast Florida would be their choice place to buy a home. Because they liked this pier, they decided to live in Atlantic Beach. Their two grown sons quit their jobs in the North and came down to join the parents. The entire Ausli family were seafood eaters and fished often. George was happy with his Italian selections and bragged around about it.

Carmelo Ausli was not at all like the gentleman, Dominick, in any way. Carmelo was a tall man with a growing belly and a good appetite. He was not a religious person, never mentioned the word "church" or "God" to anyone that I knew. If there was a lewd story going around, he knew it and insisted on telling it to anyone who would listen.

Early on, I learned that he was a man who liked to tell off-color stories about whores and sexual acts, never realizing that some people within earshot objected to blue stories. That was my only problem with him. He used to bring in black-and-white glossy photos of female pornography, which he sometimes said he photographed, and proudly passed them around. He often left these putrid pictures on the counter in the tackle shop, where I would grab them up the next morning and stuff them into empty tool drawers which lined the back wall of the shop.

George was not a voyeur and neither was Dick Poole, yet they didn't throw those things out. Maybe they thought the dirty pictures thing would pass. Poole did, however, bring it up to George that since Ausli was employed, the bait box was depleted faster than ever, and if a man is low enough to steal bait—what else might he take? George asked us to watch over our fellow employee and see if we could catch Ausli pilfering in any way, because he was still having this "goddamn leak."

Dick Poole approached Ausli on the bait problem and said that it was George who noticed the amount of bait that was taken from the chest when Ausli was on duty, and told him to let up on supplying his family with free bait. Ausli said okay. He would only take a one-half-pound package, no problem.

...

Things were running well, I thought. The first shift without Dominick at the helm was never as smooth as that time period he was there. Then he began to ask for a day or two off. George discovered that Dominick had the big C in his stomach and had to go in for radiation treatments. Of course we all finally found out that radiation was no longer effective and Dominick's time on this earth was now limited. He continued to come in for three days a week, to keep busy. Then he came for two days, and then he quit working. And a month later he died.

George was devastated. He was actually brokenhearted. I saw George cry at Dominick's funeral Mass, he was so touched.

He later told me, "Dominick was a good man. He taught me that Italians were like everybody else. There were good Italians and bad Italians, and their hearts stopped just like anybody else. It was a pleasure to have known Dominick."

21 – Ed Davis

Ed Davis "and company" were much more interesting than the Johnnie Hexton gang. For one thing, he was open for business promptly at eight o'clock in the morning without fail, and in the summer months it was ten or eleven o'clock at night before he shut down. He, too, employed an ex-convict, who was a fantastic cook and drew in a good crowd. Horace Dickerson had been caught and convicted and served time in the New Jersey State Prison for car theft when he was eighteen years of age. He said he had made the most of his incarceration by learning short-order cooking, and he also passionately took to learning the guitar. And, he said, this knowledge erased all the devious and unlawful notions he once had. He had since taught himself how to cook many other worthy dishes, especially the thick, decadent, stuffed pork chop dinners which he specialized in at Bone's Jax Beach Pier for Ed Davis.

During slow moments he joyfully entertained us all by playing his guitar in the restaurant or in the public hallway. And what a showman Horace was! He knew a lot of fast, tricky country ballads which were great crowd pleasers and he knew how to perform them with a personalized flair. Horace was a thirty-five-year-old, blue-eyed, broad-faced, middle-weight man with a good head of blond wavy hair. And he smiled a lot.

Mary Jean, his comely, dark-haired, green-eyed twenty-one-year-old girlfriend was said to come from a blue-blood New York family. She stepped in as Ed Davis' major dinner waitress. The couple made friends easily and were well liked by mostly everyone. Ed Davis was lucky to have this break of good fortune; it was not always easy to find excellent workers that were artistically talented and also pleasingly attractive.

It sure was nice not to have to see the slovenly prior group anymore. George was happy with the way business picked up, but he still pushed Ed Davis, telling him he needed to advertise his restaurant more. Ed Davis never answered, or argued with George. He would stand grinning throughout the lecture and then walk off to some project, leaving George bewildered. That was the one thing about Mr. Davis that annoyed George. He once turned to me and said, "I often wonder if I'm talking to my goddamn self."

Ed Davis listened to anyone who wanted to help him do well. His old-time friend, Charles Retig, who had a beer shack called The Last Chance Saloon, located on US Route 1 near the Palm Valley Road, came by to give some pointers. Charles Retig was an old salty guy who did little other than spend his days fishing and drinking. He came, looked around, and told Ed Davis he should sponsor a nickel-beer night, at least until he had the neighborhood familiar with the new management.

"I used to draw them into my place by offering a platter of six potato pancakes with a side of applesauce or sour cream, and three nickel beers, for one dollar. We served this from five o'clock until eight o'clock on Wednesdays. Me wife and I worked like hell, but we made out pretty good. They would eat and drink up and leave. And there were always people waiting to sit down long after seven."

But Ed Davis was not looking to give stuff away. He added potato pancakes to his menu, at his price of three dollars. And George talked him out of holding a nickel-beer night. George didn't give a reason, except to say, "Nah, that's nuts. You'd have more trouble than it's worth." That was probably reasoning enough. Davis nixed the nickel-beer night.

He did have specials, especially boiled shrimp. That is, he had it when he was able to buy decent eating-sized shrimp wholesale from George's supplier. The fried-fish sandwiches and fish chowder were very popular, and of course these were made from seafood Davis obtained from the pier, quite simply given to him most of the time.

22 – World-Record Hammerhead

My spring notes are full of delightful surprises such as: *Big fish caught today.* Starting in May, all kinds of warm-weather species begin to be caught by those who know how. By now I had learned that there are devoted fishermen who rarely catch anything. This is because they don't know how and are too blockheaded to realize this. Wise is the recreational fisherman who takes the time to learn: 1) what species is presently being caught; 2) what the popular bait is; 3) what size hook is best to use; 4) what species are on moratorium; 5) what are their legal sizes; and 6) the number of fish that one is allowed to keep. If everyone who likes to spend time fishing learns these six things, he or she will not be disappointed too often. Every tackle store and bait-selling place has all this information, or should have, I would think.

George often sent me out on the crowded pier with a box of what he called "these whiting hooks," which were small, one-half-inch wide, shiny steel hooks. I'd replace these on leaders where I found people trying to catch small surf fish like whiting and pompano with unrealistic big hooks. Some seafood varieties have small mouths and could never be caught on those monster grabbers, but may nibble away the bait without getting hooked. George was a man who liked to see everyone catching fish from his pier and was delighted when they did. I found most people were happy to be corrected, but there were always some who thought they knew more than we pier people and ignored our help. They usually went home with an empty pail.

I always told them, "You can catch big fish on a small hook, but you will not get any small panfish on those outsized hooks. If you geared up right from the start, you'd be more successful."

When I go out to get a mess of whiting and/or Florida pompanos, I personally use even a smaller salt-water number four Eagle Claw hook. This, on a fifteen-inch-long monofilament leader, is attached to a number five swivel which holds above it a free-sliding two-ounce sinker. I learned from observing successful people who usually caught what they were after. I copied what was known to work well. That's how I became more successful at catching what I was after. However, I liked George's "whiting hooks" because these were also good for catching sheepshead, catfish, butterfish, yellowtail, angelfish, perch, snapper, porgies, sea bass, grunts, croakers, and at least a hundred other small-mouthed types. However, when fishing for blues, drum, mackerel, flounder, ocean trout, and the types that have larger mouths and jaws, the hook, line, and leader should be large enough to safely hold that fish.

...

The summer months were always very exciting. A number of large kingfish were caught from the pier and a world-record shark was landed successfully. Huge ocean fish are a bit easier to handle from within a boat, especially if one is fishing from a boat that can be maneuvered to help bring in the struggling monster. But pier fishing is an entirely different situation. For one thing, the pier's pylons are naturally encrusted with live, razor-sharp barnacle-like shellfish, and I can't tell how many different kinds of seafoods I've seen cut themselves off here and scoot back into the deep. Catching big varieties from the pier is downright tricky work.

I've always been fascinated by those who caught a big kingfish from the pier. This definitely exemplified specialized fishing knowledge. The seasoned, older anglers had my respect; but fishermen such as Al Romaeo (age eighteen), Daryl Sprague (sixteen), Doug Johnson, Red Smith, and all those younger men got my admiration and adoration for how well they geared for and fought their prey. I'm talking about landing game fish weighing fifteen to twenty pounds and more, which they battled and netted safely at the pier. The late Doug Johnson was our next-door neighbor who generously shared his catch with my husband and me, and so I simply know how delicious smoked kingfish is. One summer Doug Johnson caught two kings in one day, a real bonanza!

When fishermen saw certain schools of baitfish within reach of the pier, such as mullet, porgies, or glass minnows, as Doug Johnson used to say, "It's time to put down your 'lead line' and put your king rig out there." That means the men used two rods. One for a heavy-weighted anchor line which they tossed out as far as they could and waited to see if indeed it was anchored down. If it was still dragging with the current, they brought it back in and tossed it out again until they were certain it was secured to the bottom of the sea. Most people made a gadget with a heavy piece of lead and a cut-up heavy coat hanger, which resembled a many-pronged star, that usually held well in the rolling ocean.

Onto this anchored line, Doug Johnson then sent out his king rig. The king rig must have a sturdy, large rod with an equally strong gauged reel, and with at least a quarter of a pound of twenty- or thirty-pound test Ande monofilament line. To this is added a sturdy swivel, to which is attached five feet of thin-gauged leader wire, with a double set of size two saltwater hooks. The first hook is pinned through the top fin of a live bluefish, the second through the tail fin. This floating bait is held in place with a gadget known as a spring-type wooden clothespin, which will readily detach upon a strike. Then Doug sat and confabbed with comrades as he waited until a kingfish spotted the bait. His fun began when the visitor from the deep skyrocketed out of the water and mouthed that active live bait!

The trick then, according to Doug Johnson, was not to get too darn excited and yank him in too soon. Doug always let his king run out about a hundred yards, pulling out taut line, before he turned his fish around. By the time Doug cranked him in, that noble king was too doggone tired to even see the pylons. All Doug had to do was scoop him up in his drop-net and haul him up to the deck. Of course, he then had a cooling drink and enjoyed a bit of rejoicing.

On Friday, July 4, 1975, my notes read: *Big, long, busy day at the pier, with a number of newsworthy fish caught.*

Also on this day Ed Davis superseded Mr. C. Rollin's 32-pound kingfish and Catfish Miller's 32½-pound king with his 33-pounder! This was another happy day for Ed Davis.

Next, on a quiet morning of a hot and humid day, at eleven o'clock a.m., applause broke out for Al Romaeo, for his 30-pound kingfish, and again thirty minutes later for another 25-pounder Al caught!

Bobby Brown, our cordial black man, also on this day caught a 36-inch cobia at the end of the pier while fishing on the bottom for whiting with a live shrimp. Cobia is also an incredibly great-tasting variety, so he filled his freezer compartment with cobia steaks.

On July 30, it was windy, cloudy, and rainy, and Mr. Burt McMains caught a 31-pound king; other than that, it was a quiet day concerning large fish. Then on Friday, August 1, there were three kings caught weighing in between 10 and 15 pounds each; the gang at the end of the pier called these smaller kings, "snakes." "Some snakes," I'd say, because this size is the best eating.

Nine big jacks were also tousled in on this day. Fishermen cut away the back ends of these jacks for food, but tossed the head and front end in the ocean, saying that part was wormy.

Bobby Brown again caught a huge fish, a doormat flounder. He also caught this one straight down near the pylons, with a live shrimp for bait.

On the clapboard siding above the restaurant's two doorways in the pier's open hallway was a list of two-inch-high lettered names of those men who had caught noteworthy kingfish since the time Mr. Williams ran the place. On that list appeared several names of those who had landed 60-pound kingfish. The pier of course is now long gone, but there must be pictures of that list somewhere in this world. I'm sorry to say I couldn't locate any.

...

WORLD'S RECORD HAMMERHEAD SHARK CAUGHT BY BLACKIE REASOR

Saturday night, July 5, 1975, our daily person, Blackie Reasor, subdued a monster 14' 5" hammerhead shark that weighed 706 pounds and was declared a world-record catch! It was a colossal fish.

I gave Blackie a big old trophy, for this was no easy feat. According to Doug Johnson, another shark club man who was there that night, he and the clubbers were amazed at how well Blackie played that catch. Luckily the knots on his tackle held out throughout the long battle. So many men lose their fish because of faulty equipment or poorly made knots. Blackie didn't have much in the way of real estate, but his fishing tackle could win top prize anywhere. That night, he held on to a basket-sized 16/0 reel filled with 130-pound Ande test line, and a look of definite determination.

Even now I can actually see Blackie's eyes narrow after his "clicker" went off—that's the alarm sounder when there is a pull at the bait—and as he drew his line taut and found something at the other end he immediately began his plan for its capture. Right away, he became a hard-core shark fisherman leaning back into his leather harness fighting belt, and began to crank it in.

At forty-nine years of age, the oldest of the Jacksonville Beach Shark Club, Blackie gave the club's female gallery a spectacular view of a real shark fighter that night. A dark-haired, fine-featured man of average height, Blackie stood wide-legged, with his shirt opened down to his handmade belt buckle, and with a lethal knife hanging from a sheath at his side, he showed the club's groupies he meant business.

Pretty soon it became apparent that he had an "extra big one" on. Quite a few times the fish took several hundred yards of taut line, as if the reel was on free spool. Doug Johnson said accomplices kept pouring water on Blackie's reel to keep it from burning up. Pretty soon the big predator was only able to pull a hundred yards and then less and less. But it did take Blackie an hour and twenty minutes of hard work to bring this enormous fish to the side of the pier.

Once Blackie brought his shark to the edge, there was no way to bring it up on deck, for the largest drop-net was way too small to even consider it. So Blackie had to beach the monster. He drag-pulled it the whole thousand feet along the side of the pier until it was lying on the beach nearest to First Street. Here they put a block and tackle up on the south side of the pier's entrance boardwalk and pulled the hammerhead shark up until the beast stood on its nose, where it soon died.

After it was professionally weighed and charted at Monty's Marina in Mayport, Blackie ripped open its belly and removed twelve live babies via cesarean operation. That was a lucky surprise. Doug Johnson said Blackie reluctantly presented his fellow shark fishermen with one of those babies as a token of appreciation for their help. There were several opinions that the idea never occurred first with

Blackie, but because of the worthy catch the men jointly thought they deserved a baby for their next shark bait, and so Blackie was finally convinced to part with most of them.

July 5, 1975: Blackie Reasor shows his 706-pound world-record monster hammerhead shark caught on Bone's Jax Beach Pier. His weaponry tackle was an 11-foot surf rod equipped with a huge 16/0 Penn reel, loaded with 130-pound Ande test line. Admiring fellow shark clubbers said Reasor heroically withstood the long fight, as did the many perfect knots he had made to extend his line.

Blackie never went to bed that night, for he was sitting on the long bench in the pier's hallway sipping coffee when I arrived at seven o'clock, and the very first thing he said to me, even before a morning greeting, was, "Ms. Eve, I'm going to be famous all over the world."

"Have you already heard for certain that you have the record?"

"No, not yet, but I know I have it."

"Well then, my congratulations, sir."

"Thank ya, thank ya, thank ya, ma'am."

He was so joyous, he was almost sparking fire despite the fact that he was physically spent.

Blackie's shark-fishing friends helped him find a taxidermist experienced with fish, who was willing to work with him. There was a certain amount of expense which Blackie had no idea he'd have if and when he ever caught a world-record shark. He called himself a "contractor," but in all the time I've known him I never heard of him in the actual role of a contractor; he was always fishing. His family of four lived in a one-room apartment over a storefront. His wife, Phyllis, worked at the pier's restaurant and seemed to be the sole supporter for their two children, one a new baby.

Blackie spent the next day or two receiving plaudits and good-luck wishes from crowds of strangers visiting the pier. He spoke with them as if they were blood relatives. Perhaps he considered one of them might turn out to be his angel benefactor.

It was hard to tell who Blackie was talking business with. At one time he told me he was in conference with the Hollywood star, Lucille Ball, and her company. Another time he was "dealing" with a "rich New Yorker," and still another day he was "signing with someone with a lot of money from Mexico and would soon embark on a world tour." Blackie wanted so much to become famous and wealthy. But first he needed seed money, not only for the taxidermist but also for a much-needed fresh wardrobe beyond flip-flops and old shorts. Gas money and hotel costs for travel expenses also had to be considered. But, as they said, he didn't own a pot to pee in or a doorway to throw it out from. All he could do under the circumstances was to wish for a miracle.

I remember asking George why he wasn't at least a little bit interested in Blackie's need for capital. "For the amount I hear you're spending at the dog track, that same money invested in his shark may pay off better than the dogs. Ever think of that, George?"

Georges' eyes narrowed and he answered me in the strangest way. He threw a North Carolina "Georgism" at me and I'm still trying to figure it out.

He said, "If you loan somebody your horse, and if that n— don't give him an ear of corn, you don't loan him anymore."

George never discussed Blackie's plight with me beyond that much. Dick Poole told me that Blackie had owed George quite a bit of money for many years.

…

For a few days after the record-breaking shark was caught, the pier made quite a bit of money from the "walkers" who merely visited without fishing there. I suppose many of them came thinking the shark was still at the pier, or maybe they were content to visit the place where the shark had been caught. Hundreds of dollars were taken in from these sightseers. But after a couple of days the crowd and the excitement was over, at least for us employees.

Blackie managed to raise some traveling money as soon as the taxidermist announced he was finished with the shark. We heard that one of the big boys, such as the Ande Monofilament Company, came through with a contribution.

Blackie wore a brand-new leather harness and shiny new boots and had a fresh haircut. But what surprised me was the new pickup truck and carrier that was delivered to pull his gorgeously lacquered hammerhead. I never heard Blackie's explanation as to who was responsible for that. Fishermen thought it was the taxidermist who had enough invested and hoped something would turn up so he could get his money for his work.

All duded up in new threads and with a pocketful of spending money, Blackie went off on a two-week tour around the state of Florida.

He had found an agent who had made plans and a schedule where Blackie was to visit men's clubs, schools, and all sorts of club meetings around Florida. He planned to befriend everyone on his journey. Everybody and his brother would know Blackie Reasor and his world-record hammerhead through his educational lecture, he told me. He tried his prattle out on me for several days.

Hello, I'm Blackie Reasor. Here's the world's record hammerhead shark I caught off the Bone's Jacksonville Beach Pier this past summer. It weighed 706 pounds and measured fourteen feet, five inches long.

All sharks have a torpedo-shaped body for swift movement. But the hammerhead, as you can observe, has this crossbar-shaped head. Its head grows sideways until it looks like a hammer, and is so named. Its eyes are situated out on the ends of the hammer, giving this species a peculiar, ominous look. My shark took almost two hours to land, and I used a 16.0-sized reel.

As you can see, their coloring is gray on top and paling nearer to the belly. Their skin is covered with minute tooth-like scales called denticles, giving it a sandpaper-like feeling when touching the shark. Its teeth are also of the same dentine material, and the beast has several rows of big teeth at all times. When one row wears out, there is another fresh row beneath, ready to use.

Hammerheads (Sphyrnidae), like other sharks, are different animals from whales and porpoises because they are fish, with gills, (the others are mammals). This is a nervous, roving beast of prey that thrives in all warm waters of the world's seas. It breeds alive, and feeds on other fish, especially dogfish, rays, and other sharks. Carnivorous, it will eat its own babies if they were able to be caught. This shark will attack anything in the water that looks edible, and for that reason they are considered to be dangerous to man.

Like all sharks, the meat is edible, and there are no bones. Its skeleton is composed of cartilage. Our Jacksonville Beach Shark Club often has a barbecue of shark steaks after our day is done. Shark meat tastes wonderful. I suggest you all try tasting shark meat at least one time; you may discover you like it very much. Thank you for coming.

They are allowing me a couple of minutes here, so if there are any questions, I'm ready for you.

...

After we cut a bunch of stuff out, I told Blackie that this amount of information was plenty long enough. He had a couple of pages more to say with all sorts of encyclopedia data, but I told him he would feel awful if they stopped him in the middle of his speech, asking questions. He was not a trained storyteller, though his attitude was positive. If he memorized this short speech, and had their full attention, he'd do real well, we thought. Burt McMains and I convinced Blackie that any time left in his allotment could be spent answering questions.

Everybody I knew wished Blackie good luck and hoped he'd find happiness in his new exposure. So, off he went on a two-week tour.

…

Next thing I learned, when he got back from his trial run, everything had disappeared. The truck and carrier were nowhere in sight and even the shark was nowhere to be seen. Oddly enough we didn't see Blackie sitting around in the hallway either. *How weird,* I thought.

When finally I saw Blackie and asked what happened, he muttered, "Oh, the investor has things to work out before I can travel again," and he walked off not wanting to talk further.

Dick Poole said Blackie was now legally tied up until he paid up. Dick added, "The taxidermist was still waiting for his first penny as a payment, as well as other people. I doubt it will ever develop further because Blackie is not willing to let anyone in on the deal. He is not willing to give someone a percentage for their investment. Yet he hasn't anything, either. So there you are. How can you do business with a stone?" Poole laughed at Blackie's situation.

Legally, things dangled for a little while, until Blackie's record catch was broken by a new hammerhead record that weighed more than a thousand pounds. That, sadly, was the end of Blackie ever becoming rich and famous.

His world-record hammerhead shark was donated to the Jacksonville Children's Museum, and that was the end of Blackie's big dream. It was sad to see this man deflated so badly.

Robert L. Williams on his daily health stroll back and forth across the pier, until he felt he had a good workout.

Bill Jackson, the handyman, hoses down the ripe-smelling Miss Piggy, George Bone's intended pier mascot.

Peg Santas, operator of Ann's Gift Shop, shows a customer an artist's view of a Florida panther in natural light, outside the shop.

A nine-foot shark, caught in the wee hours of the morning, awaits the fisherman's return from his coffee break. He will weigh, record, and remove the trophy jaws, and release the carcass back to the ocean for crab food.

From left, some of the pier's best young fishermen: Red, John, Felix, and Al. These kids really knew how to catch 'em!

Seashell seekers below the pier, looking for specimens early in the morning.

The pier opened at sunrise, when the day was still quiet and uneventful.

Pvt. Daryl Sprague, whose mother was a longtime cook on the pier, came here to fish during his first US Army furlough.

Mr. Bone's crew, hired for the day, help replace one of the pier's worn-out pilings. Bone is beneath the deck in the surf, guiding the heavy timber. Once it's in place, the tide and gravity will take it down to bedrock.

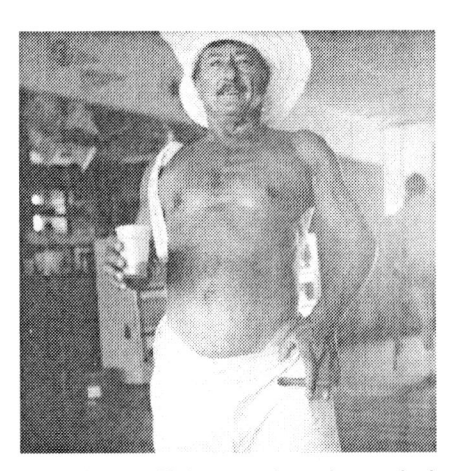

George Bone drinking his pacifying ambrosia early in the day. I tried to get through to him to no avail, saying that too much alcohol would shorten his life. He told me to mind my own business. Another time he told me he simply had to have some strong bourbon to quiet his jagged nerves.

Pie-eyed and ranting, George Bone is on his knees with a cigar in this mouth, just yelling for attention.

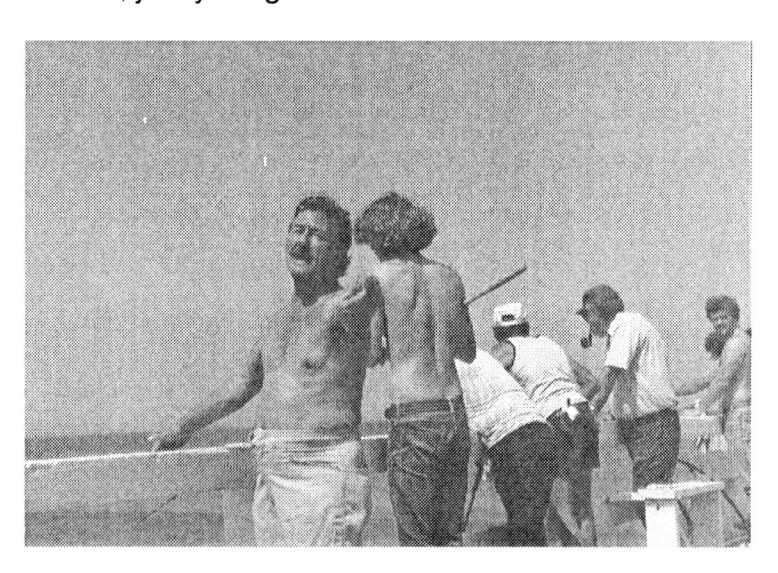

Often, when we saw George Bone on the pier, he was yelling at someone or something.

George Bone playfully lifts the leg of a regular customer in a show of affection, while Mario's friend looks on with quizzical amusement. These two men, like me, were frustrated not knowing how to get through to George.

Mrs. George Bone sets up a makeshift table with fresh flowers and cake for her dear husband's 55th birthday. Fishermen and women were invited.

Richard Rogerson and his Slurpee stand manager, Virginia, with George butting in.

Flocks of grackles and cowbirds come to the fishing pier to steal bait from the fishermen.

George Bone yelling at someone. He didn't seem to know how to speak softly.

Mike Boyer fights off a bait-grabbing grackle that is after his fresh shrimp.

Doug Johnson shows off his trophy. This bull shark was big enough to swallow Doug whole.

A visitor from Georgia shows off his flounder.

Bert McMains admires the author's catch.

Larry Finch, owner of Northeast Seafood Shop, with his future wife, Marilyn Murphy, showing off their morning's catch.

Dal Rollins with another sea trout.

Blackie Reasor with two of his smaller fish.

TV Channel 4's Paul Cameron shows off his catch to friends.

Rhonda's young son lifts his heavy kingfish onto the gaff board, so proud he was of that big catch.

Larry Finch with his sea trout.

Muriel Rogerson's dad, Millard Roberts, in his retirement years became a kingfish expert.

Eve Bates, pier employee, exhibits her sea trout and a snakelike ribbon fish. She will only cook the trout. The other will be used as kingfish bait.

Coolie Baker, George Bone's cousin from North Carolina, proudly displays his sizeable sea trout.

Bert McMains heads home with his flounder catch. His wife will stuff those fillets with crabmeat, and they will rejoice with their fresh seafood banquet.

Rhonda Wilson's young son proudly shows off his lonesome catch.

The pier's new manager, Rhonda Wilson, looks on as Larry Finch prepares a freshly caught trout for the tackle shop's spider (frying pan).

Eve Bates congratulates Mike Chakos for successfully landing his terrifyingly big bull shark.

Dal Rollins 1978 Kingfish Tournament celebration gang. From left: 1) Larry Finch, 2) Marilyn Murphy, 3) Dal Rollins, 4) Bill Jackson and his girlfriend, 5) son of Rhonda Wilson, 6) John Ballinger, 7) Little Blackie and 8) Big Blackie Reasor, 9) Jake Brown, and 10) Rhonda Wilson with her darling little daughter. The unnumbered folks are unknown.

A visitor exhibits his beautiful kingfish. Fishermen refer to these young, slender kings as "snakes."

Blackie Reasor with a little shark and a dozen pan-sized weakfish—a good morning's catch.

The author with her favorite seafood, the incredible-tasting red bass.

The author with her noble speckled sea trout.

George Bone spins his tales with a friend after he unclogs the pier's sewage system.

The pier crowd on April 12, 1981, when the first launch of the space shuttle was clearly seen blasting off into the wild blue yonder of space, from the Kennedy Space Center.

Jim Glass came on his fast two wheels to find fish.

Ray Holt, the pickled Canadian pier employee, trying to look harmless.

On a clear summer's day, the pier filled up with fishermen and sightseers.

Cherokee Chief Clyde Haymaker, of North Georgia, came annually to find fish here.

Big Blackie and Little Blackie Reasor arrive early in the day to have their breakfast at the pier's restaurant.

Thelma Panther, a Seminole madonna, visits the pier with her offspring.

Entrepreneur Jake Brown, operator of the pier's restaurant, looks out at the heavy downpour, wondering if he should close shop for the day.

Pier employee Scott Wood, with John Ballinger, Blackie Reasor, and Richard Rogerson, overseeing work on the pier.

23 – Celebrities

For the first few days following Blackie Reasor's world-record catch, the pier had a constant parade of visitors all day long, from mid-morning until closing time. Many of them were looking for Blackie to shake his hand or to ask a question about sharks and their ways.

Blackie told me he was approached by the Hollywood star, Lucille Ball, and her party, but I'm not sure that is correct because he was known to tell bold-faced untruths. As far as I know, Ms. Ball did not make herself known to me or anyone in charge, so who knows whether that was true?

However, some celebrities did come and chat with us during that time. I remember greeting Shaun Cassidy, the young son of actors Shirley Jones and Jack Cassidy, who came up on the pier with a couple of pals, when his band, VIRGIN, was on tour locally. I remember wishing him and his band much success. Shaun and his companions responded appreciatively, with much smiling along with their pleasant thank-yous. I couldn't resist telling him that I, too, was a Virgo, born in mid-September, to which his warm response was: "Aw-right! Here, have one of my guitar picks!" From his pants pocket he handed me an inscribed guitar pick—which is still wedged in between the glass and frame of the picture hanging in my den.

One day George and I were at the front counter when we noticed a black lady standing alone at the back door, looking out onto the activity on the pier. At first we thought she was waiting for a companion who might still have been on the way.

It was George who first recognized her as a TV star and shouted out a greeting: "Good morning, Esther Rolle. How are you, this fine day?"

"Good morning to you too," she responded as she approached the counter while pulling out her change purse from deep in her décolleté. "I'd like to rent a fishing pole with bait, please. I'd like to catch a fish today," she timidly revealed.

"Yes, ma'am, we'll fix you right up to catch a fish. What do you want to catch today, a bluefish, or maybe a flounder?"

George picked a rod that was light in weight and equipped with a new spinner reel, and he put a fresh whiting hook on the leader for her.

"If you hook into a sizeable flounder, don't pull it up out of the water because you might lose it. Call us and we will come with a drop-net and get it up for you," George informed Ms. Rolle.

"I have never caught a flounder," she admitted.

"Then you must fish with live bait and you might catch one," George instructed as he graciously went out to catch a half dozen live shrimp from the live-bait tank.

"How do I hook on a live shrimp?"

With that, George knew she was not experienced enough to fish with live bait.

"Eve, here, will take you out there and set you up."

I was sent out to help Ms. Rolle catch a flounder. We spent an hour and a half or so with this celebrity, talking about the weather, fishing, and favorite foods. She said she loved fish and had it a couple times each week. She did not catch anything but a couple of fat bluefishes. She was happy to catch anything. However, she didn't care to take them home, and offered her catch to some neighboring black people, who also rejected this offer. An Asian lady saw this and asked for Ms. Rolle's fish and was glad to have them.

George said that black people, as a rule, did not use bluefish and considered this species as "trash fish," along with ladyfish and ocean catfish.

This surprised me. Back in New Jersey, as soon as the snapper blues showed up plentifully in the spring, "Bluefish Specials" showed up in most shore restaurants and were greatly sought after.

I learned something new every day on the fishing pier.

…

One day I looked towards the entrance and thought I saw Mutt and Jeff from the comics page coming up the boardwalk. It was my six-foot-four-inch husband walking with a little short guy who looked familiar. As they drew closer I saw he was with the Hollywood actor,

Mickey Rooney! I later learned that they had just met at the foot of the pier, but they were chatting away like old friends.

And no sooner was Mickey Rooney up under the shade of the pier-house than he began speaking to everybody he saw. George and his wife thought Mickey Rooney was an especially sociable individual; my husband, a professional sales representative, had him pegged that day as one who was stomping for business. Mr. Rooney was in a play at the Alhambra Dinner Theatre and that was what he talked about because he wanted to see more people there.

As he walked up to me he said, "Hello, I'm Mickey Rooney. I'm down here at the Alhambra in a play called *See How They Run*. Here is a ticket for a house discount. Come on over. I'll see you there?" He waited for a response.

I have to admit that he sold me and my husband, along with George and Ann Bone. The play was one of those I saw and soon forgot. It was not in a class with, for instance, *The Immoralist*, by Billy Rose. We had seen that play in Philadelphia in the early 1940s and it left me with strong memories. I can still *picture* James Dean stalking his lover in the orchard. The only thing I really remember from Mickey Rooney's stage play is Rooney's running leap, which appeared rather awkward at the time. Other than that, it was forgettable.

…

George once told me he had met many Hollywood celebrities on his pier but couldn't remember any of their names when we talked about notables, except for old man John Carradine and Martha Raye.

"Carradine suffered from the same type of arthritis as my wife. His hands, like Ann's, were gnarled and distorted. And that Martha Raye woman!" George laughed as he recalled meeting Ms. Raye, and he said, "She soaked up most of my booze when she was up here."

George was not as enamored of celebrities as most people. I often wondered what they thought when they met our captain of this fishing pier.

…

One morning on my way to work, I met Mr. Hugh O'Brien on the beach. Linwood and I then lived at the corner of Thirteenth Avenue S. and Second Street. It happened that Hugh O'Brien and his household had rented an oceanfront cottage on Twelfth Avenue S., so it was natural that we would run into each other during that time.

One fine morning as I descended the pathway through the rocks to the beach, there sat this handsome young man adjusting the collar on the most beautiful white German shepherd I had ever seen. The dog's fur was gleaming and well brushed.

"Good morning, sir. What an attractive dog you have here," I said as they made room for me to climb down.

"Thank you. This is Bear," the attractive man responded.

"Hello, Bear, are you enjoying the beach this morning?" I asked as I feather-touched the dog's nose on my final step down.

"And I'm Hugh O'Brien," he offered.

"Howdy," I said. "Are you the actor, Hugh O'Brien?"

"Yes. I'm in a production called *Cactus Flower*, which is playing at the Alhambra Dinner Theatre. Come see me if you can," he said.

"Okay. When would be the most magical performance?" I teased.

Mr. O'Brien thought a long moment and then he really did give me a date which he thought would be his best night, and he even told me why. But due to other commitments my husband and I didn't get to see Mr. O'Brien in *Cactus Flower*, unfortunately. I can remember his athletic face struggling to figure out that magical date, and best of all I remember the friendly face of his pal, Bear. I swear that dog actually had a smile on its face for me.

When I got to the pier, I told George about meeting the charming Hugh O'Brien and his fantastic Bear, but George's comment deflated me when he yelled, "So what? What does that O'Brien guy have that I don't have? He has a goddamn dog that shits turds on our beach, that's what!" He took another slug of bourbon and disappeared into the poolroom.

…

One of the most interesting people who visited the pier when I was on duty was not exactly a known fisherman or a glamorous movie star or TV celebrity. It was Ross Allen, a man from the wilds of Florida. "Wild" is how I remember him, since my husband and I first met Ross Allen back in 1950 when we spent some time vacationing near Silver Springs, Florida, where Mr. Allen started his illustrious career as a herpetologist.

On this day he was researching places to invest in. He had heard a rumor that this pier was up for sale and he wanted to know more about it. I told him that this was news to me but George would be in any minute, and I invited Mr. Allen to sit down inside the tackle shop.

We began a conversation when I told him I remembered that early in his career he served as the stand-in for the brawny, good-looking Johnny Weissmuller when a Tarzan movie was produced at Silver Springs.

"Yes, ma'am," he agreed, "that was back when I had all my body parts and much more hair."

I giggled at his personal humor.

It was at Silver Springs that my husband and I first saw him "milk a rattlesnake." His show was set up on a glazed table placed under the shade of a giant oak tree. We were close enough to see the two big fangs of the rattler being pushed against the inside of a clear glass vial, and we saw the milky venom squirt against the glass and run into a small bottle below it.

We later talked with young Ross Allen while sitting under the shade of another oak, and when he heard we were from New Jersey he told us he had relocated here from his birthplace of Pittsburgh, Pennsylvania, to be nearer to wild places where he could find snakes throughout most of the year. As a budding herpetologist, he said, it was important to be near snakes, especially since he wanted to collect and sell snake venom. We asked how he got so many rattlers which we saw in his snake pen, and he said he caught most of them himself because he was "too poor to pay someone to round them up."

"How did you round up rattlesnakes?" asked my curious business major husband, who was about the same age as Ross Allen.

He told us he caught most of them during the hot weather of summer when they were mostly above ground. He said he'd find a large open field of about twenty or thirty acres and park his car in the middle of that field, preferably near a brook. Then he'd take a nap for an hour or so. He went back in the heat of midafternoon and, with his snake stick, drag out and bag the critters that were curled up and enjoying the shade under his car. A one-hundred-degree day was nearly always productive, he said.

"Rattlesnakes can smell the shade and will move towards it until they find it." According to Ross Allen, "Rattlesnakes will die if the thermometer reaches one hundred ten degrees Fahrenheit. They simply cannot tolerate that kind of heat." Having learned this made it easier for him to know where and how to find them. "I'd always come back with a couple of big ones," he explained. "Then there were people who called in for help to get a snake out of their garage or from the corner of their patio. The police also called me for help, so I collected rattlesnakes from all sources."

The next time I saw Ross Allen was about 1973, when I took a visiting friend from New Jersey to the St. Augustine Alligator Farm, where Allen was now relocated after selling out his holdings at Silver Springs. At the St. Augustine Alligator Farm he had a fancy redwood-and-glass studio filled with a couple dozen squirming, rattling, diamondback rattlesnakes.

He entered the glass house which stood above the crowd of spectators, and caught and milked a snake in full view. I remember commenting to Betty Moring, my visiting friend, how intimate Allen was with that battalion of snakes squirming in that show cabin. How close his feet and hands got to some of them, which were in striking position. It so happened that he was bitten soon after our visit.

"This sixteenth bite nearly killed me," he told me that day at Bone's Pier.

I took his right hand into mine and examined his thumb, which was where the fangs caught him and caused him so much trouble. A gangrenous infection from the rattler's venom permanently destroyed the structure of his first digit. Except for a small point on one side, there was no nail and no padded thumb tissue down as far as the first joint. I shuddered to think of this man's painful suffering ... this good man who had saved so many lives from snakebite.

On that day at the pier, Ross Allen hung around for a good hour before George arrived, and we talked about how scarce snook and some other varieties of fish were beginning to be, and about the new state laws that were beginning to list about every variety we have here in the Florida surf.

Allen seemed to be well versed on the world's problems and especially regarding the ocean's plight. I remember his whole being exhibited new energy when he began saying something to this effect: "If the world's communities don't stop the acidification of our seas, with the outlandish amounts of industrial waste materials being dumped daily into our oceans, there will come a day when we will all hunger for a fish sandwich."

That pier visit with Ross Allen took place twenty-eight years ago, and not only has he long departed, but as I am reporting this story the laws are changing fast. I see that his prophesy has already come into effect. At that time the extremely common snapper blues were not yet on moratorium, but today (2013), it is illegal to catch bluefish under 12 inches in Florida waters. We also have to be very careful with every fish we catch, because another variety may be on the forbidden list! And the fines are horrific.

My favorite panfish, the Florida pompano, must be a minimum of 11 inches, and only six allowed per person per day. Flounder here must be a minimum of 12 inches; sheepshead, a minimum of 12 inches; black drum must be a minimum of 14 inches and maximum of 24 inches; red drum, a minimum of 18 inches and a maximum of 27 inches, a window of only 10 inches when they are legal. And when I go out on a boat to do some deep-sea fishing, I have to be equally as careful because they have closed season on some varieties such as red and vermillion snappers. The once-plentiful king mackerel must be a minimum of 24 inches measured from nose to fork of the tail.

Prior to fishing, I'd earnestly advise everyone to check things out with www.MyFWC.com/marine for current regulations.

I simply can't forget my conversation with Ross Allen. His words on acidifying the world's oceans keep ringing in my ears like a sharp bell.

***

Informational

A fifteen-foot eastern diamondback rattlesnake was caught in St. Johns County in 2011. It was the largest on record ever caught. After seeing this, I did a little research and learned the following:

One bite from a snake this large contains enough venom to kill over forty full-grown men.

The head alone is larger than the hand of a large-sized man.

This snake was probably alive when Gen. Dwight Eisenhower was president.

A bite from those fangs would equal being penetrated by two 1/4-inch screwdrivers.

A snake this size could easily maul a child.

A snake this size has an approximately accurate six-foot striking distance. (The distance for an average-size rattlesnake is about two feet.)

This snake weighed 170 pounds. That is exactly what I weigh.

**

THE JANET STANCELL MEETING

One of my fondest memories regarding celebrities is the day I met Janet Stancell on the beach, while on my way to work. I thought something looked vaguely familiar about her plumpish person and when she caught me looking at her, I greeted her with a cheerful good morning. I was immediately invited to help identify a slipper shell. We began chatting and she introduced herself as Janet Stancell, a newcomer to this beach.

When I learned she was originally from Snyder, New York, I told her that my husband's first company transfer by the Hamilton Watch Company had been to Buffalo, New York, from our home in Haddonfield, New Jersey, in 1954, and we had settled in Snyder. I asked where she resided there. She said they were on Kings Highway. "For goodness sakes," I said, "we were close neighbors back then. We were on the forefront of Campus Drive."

I still didn't know who she really was. However, we discovered we both had raised two daughters; we both used to go to Kleinhans Music Hall, and we both enjoyed Buffalo's famous sandwich, the (roast) "beef on a weck" (kummelweck) roll. We found plenty to talk about, but I told her I had to get to work on the pier and invited her up there whenever she had time and we would continue our reminiscing about Snyder.

As it turned out, Janet Stancell was a troubled individual. She walked the beach for an hour or more every day to keep her mind at peace, she said. Within two days of our meeting on the beach, she parked her car at the pier's parking lot. She came up to see me and we went into the restaurant to have a cup of coffee. At this time, I learned she had moved out of the William E. Stancell home a month before, was now living at the hotel, and was waiting for her divorce to come through.

Janet was no longer a young person. Nor was she greatly attractive with her large, plain face. She had to be sixty-five or more, according to her sagging jowl line. Her hair was dyed black, or nearly black, and it mismatched her faded eyebrows. Her long, thick hair was piled on top of her head, giving her a bouffant appearance. Her thin, white skin and lusterless eyes against the dyed hair gave way to what she might have thought was a safe secret.

It was plainly seen that Janet was eager to find new friends. After she relocated to Jacksonville Beach with Mr. Stancell, she said she had visited every library within a hundred miles.

"Librarians are the most gracious people!" she exclaimed. "One never knows when we might need their help."

After her previous husband died, she said she was drying up from loneliness. She decided to take a cruise. There she met Mr. Stancell. They danced well together and, for a brief time, had lots of fun and laughter. As soon as he found out she was the popular millionaire authoress known as Taylor Caldwell, with more than three dozen top-selling books to her credit, he proposed marriage. Foolishly, she accepted his proposal and actually married him. And all too soon she found herself in trouble. She was wed only a short time, about a year, to Stancell, a retired Jacksonville Beach real estate developer, and she was already anxiously awaiting a divorce.

She said she was not able to live with someone who was so childishly inviting himself into every corner of her privacy. This man, she said, insisted on answering her phone calls, making her appointments, and choosing her foods. He wanted to know about every minute of her day. She claimed the old man used to stand against her bathroom door and listen to the water run. She simply had to put an end to all those annoyances.

"I miss Marcus terribly," she told me more than once during our coffee clutches. She could not help but tell me about Marcus Reback, her previous husband with whom she was happily married for forty years. Marcus died in 1971. My body shook with tremors of danger when I saw how little time she had taken before finding a new husband.

Janet proceeded to tell me about Marcus and their home life in Buffalo, and how well they had lived. They had "patches of blooming flowers all over" their side yard. They had clusters of Shasta daisies, canna lilies, and brightly colored peonies.

Then came her words, almost in a whisper: "I keep in contact with Marcus," she said with a straight face and without any kind of warning.

"Excuse me?" I answered. Because she had used these words, I thought this lady was no longer operating on all cylinders and was losing her mind.

"May I tell you a little story?" Janet said.

She began by telling me that among their plant choices was a clump of Persian lilacs which Marcus had planted more than twenty-five years ago. The bush had developed into at least twenty healthy green stalks, but had never thrown a single bloom. Marcus and Janet thought they had planted a male of the species and had given up hope of ever seeing anything more.

Then Marcus fell into serious ill health and he told Janet, "After I die I shall see, if I can, what is wrong with that lilac bush. And if it is possible I will make it bloom for you."

"Guess what?" Janet asked me. "Marcus died, and when that spring rolled around our lilac bush was absolutely full of fragrant blooms, for the very first time since its existence!" And after a hesitant pause, Janet declared, "Because of this phenomenon I have since taken up a new study. I am now researching reincarnation."

After this last meeting, Janet disappeared from Jacksonville Beach and found her way to other climes. Subsequently, several years later I learned through a newspaper article that Taylor Caldwell, the novelist, had found a new romance with a younger man, a Canadian, and they were reportedly living in the New England area.

Now that I am working on my fourth literary project I find myself thinking about Janet Stancell every now and again. Was there a purpose behind the way she briefly came into my life?

And I wonder if there is anything to that reincarnation stuff ....

24 – Bone's Sister Comes to the Pier

One fine day, a healthy-looking, matronly lady walked up to the tackle counter and stopped me from asking if I could be of help by putting her finger against her mouth and pointing to George, who was gazing out onto the pier in deep thought. She stood there staring at him, now wearing a big smile on her lips. I began to smile at her because I could tell she was family. She had the very same blue eyes as George and the same facial bone structure.

George must have felt someone looking at him. He turned directly to the person at the counter and his eyes popped out.

"Well, hello, sis!"

He beamed as he bolted out the tackle gate and grabbed her up in a bear hug. A customer was behind sis, waiting to be admitted to the fishing pier, so George pulled her into the tackle shop and behind the tackle display wall where they embraced again.

So, this must be the sister that has recently relocated from North Carolina to North Jacksonville, where she has opened a beauty salon and is known to be doing well. George had told me about this sister, but he didn't introduce her to me that day. I don't know why, except that he probably didn't know any better.

Apparently sis had heard from the grapevine that a divorce was in progress and she had come to see what was going on, because I heard her say, "You have something important to tell me?"

And for reasons of his own George answered her, saying, "No, sis, I have nothing important to tell you."

"Are you certain?"

"Yes."

"That's good news, Georgie, because we have enough family problems as it is."

They both broke out into a weeping spell which lasted several moments. I felt close to tears myself, thinking how George and his sister were still in mourning for brother Leaston, besides suffering deep empathy and unrequited love for the brother being held in prison.

After this visit, George was into heavier drinking again, and Ann was getting more serious about filing for divorce.

This was about the time I was ready to quit because the job was no longer fun for me. But somehow, I listened to Richard Rogerson and to Ann Bone, who urged me to stay on.

25 – George Pins a Visitor to the Deck

Now for diversion, George was throwing that knife again, practicing his aim. On this particular day he took out a new specimen, a Bowie knife named for its reputed inventor, Col. James "Jim" Bowie (1796–1836). This is a stout, straight, no-nonsense, single-edged hunting knife which we stocked in the showcase and sold to fishermen as well as to hunters.

George began amusing himself by playing darts with this sharp knife. He used to stand with his back to the front counter in the tackle shop and aim at a mark he put on the back wall over the sink, and tried to make a bulls-eye throwing at it. I have to admit he was pretty darn good with that knife, and he knew it too. Eight or nine times out of ten he would be on the mark.

Often he would walk out of the tackle shop door onto the pier and throw the knife at natural marks he saw in the wooden deck. He used to do this especially whenever he knew there was a hunter or two fishing on the pier and, by golly the next thing I knew, he had sold a knife to such a visitor.

One sunny morning George was out on the deck of the pier practicing with a fresh knife when Leon Borkowski came aboard. Leon didn't pay for fishing fees, but said he only wanted to speak to George a minute. He stepped out onto the pier's deck and headed for where George was practicing with his Bowie knife. George saw him coming, and I watched as he took aim at Borkowski's feet.

I thought, *My God, George, don't try it, don't try it!*

But he did throw that knife—and pinned Borkowski to the deck!

I thought, *What a marksman he is! Look at that. George has Borkowski stuck to the pier with the Bowie knife sticking straight up through the guy's sandal.*

Then I saw the red blood spurting up. Borkowski saw it too and with his mouth wide open, he dropped to the deck in a dead faint.

George looked on with a surprised disbelief. But only for a second. George pulled up his knife and dragged Borkowski into the tackle shop where he ordered me to pour a bottle of peroxide, followed by ice, on the man's foot. George passed a glass of whiskey back and forth under the gasping man's nose. Borkowski sat up, looked about, saw his toe spurting blood, and again dropped into a faint. George tried passing his whiskey again. I mopped Borkowski's face with cold water, and he came back. Then he laughed. It was more like a nervous giggle, but it was certainly not what I'd expected.

I thought, *By golly! George and Ann will not have to worry over pier mortgage payments much longer if Borkowski finds the right lawyer.*

George helped put him into the pier's wheelchair and off they went toward the car and Beaches Hospital. Borkowski was still silently giggling as they departed.

I never saw George Bone look more sober than at that moment. It turned out better than could have been hoped for, because the knife had merely severed the shallow web between the two smallest toes and opened some blood vessels which, while bloody and frightening, did no large damage. I never heard anything more, but I soon found out that Borkowski had a lifelong fishing permit from that day on, and as far as I know he never did consult with a lawyer. It remained a mystery as to what Borkowski had on his mind when he first came to the pier.

Speaking of lawyers and such, it was about this same time that the Bones went to court and lucked out on a suit brought on by a fisherwoman who had tripped and fallen on the pier and had broken her nose on one of the uprights. I remember George had taken her to the hospital and paid for her doctor bills. But still she sued George. After the judge heard how the Bones had taken care of this person, the female judge thought they were good folks and told the suing woman so, dismissing the case. George's lawyer never presented a bill, but settled for a free fishing permit for her family of several boys.

26 – The Kindergarten Class

One morning a young kindergarten teacher brought her class to visit the pier. She had at least twenty-three bright-eyed little people full of happy wonderment. They appeared on Monday, May 19, and I granted them permission to visit the pier.

At first George was somewhere out of sight. He was probably whistling to someone in the poolroom, as he often was doing that. However, he reappeared when this bunch of little folk were stepping outside of the pier tackle shop. Right away they started to crowd together, and I could see that some of them were afraid of the loud swooshing noises coming from the noisy, rolling, high-tide surf below the deck. Their teacher saw this and immediately gathered the frightened to her and began to explain and soothe her charges.

Now, George saw this group and realized the teacher was on a field trip and he decided on the spot to make things exciting for them.

He rushed forward and greeted the teacher with a "Hello, ma'am! Let me show you where I'm about to build my dream home, on top of this pier."

The teacher had her own busy thoughts and was slow to recognize the man was in a strange world of his own. Before she knew what he was up to, George had started the line moving up the narrow stairs to the roof of the pier.

"Hurry up, come on, climb faster," he yelled to the little ones.

And they responded to his directions. Some boys and girls gleefully scooted up that steep ladder. But when they reached the roof and saw the vast ocean moving below them, they panicked. A number of kids refused to climb, so George grabbed them up bodily and one after the other, rushed them screaming and protesting up to the roof until he had all of them up there. He was perspiring profusely. The teacher was yelling for him to quit, but he didn't hear her pleas. Finally he realized that the kids were not enjoying what he wanted them to see. He was up there trying to guide them around further, but they were all frozen into a lump and crying loudly.

I could hear the commotion above me and went out from the tackle shop to see what was going on. What I saw would scare any mother on this earth! Those little kids were petrified and crying, and so now was their teacher.

"GEORGE!" I screamed. "PLEASE COME DOWN WITH THOSE STUDENTS. RIGHT NOW!"

George heard me and saw my horrified expression. He started the descent and found he had to carry nearly every one of those novices down that skinny ladder. They were simply too panicked to move. When at last he had all of them back on the deck, he looked like he was about to have a heart attack; he was wet with perspiration and red in the face.

He tried to make conversation with the teacher, but she wasn't interested in lingering further with drunken George. She pushed, pulled, collected, and counted her class and hurriedly departed. The students never saw more of the beach. It was a peculiar field trip for them, to say the least. It could have been a catastrophe. I'm glad they got down safely. I never saw them ever again.

27 – Horace and Olive Arrive

I can't recall when Horace and Olive arrived at our pier. They must have already had their gear and didn't need anything except for bait. Somebody else might have admitted them. I learned a lot from the folks I welcomed aboard, especially those who came desiring to fish and wanting to buy their equipment rather than rent a fishing pole. This gave us a little time together to get to know each other. This type of customer usually came from far-off places, often from some northern burg and wanted to tell us their name and where they came from, and many times a whole lot more than that.

I became aware of this couple as another of the regular daily customers who showed up a little after ten in the morning and were aboard until late afternoon, leaving the pier at four or five o'clock. I learned from another pier worker that Horace and Olive returned nearly every evening to fish by moonlight. Quite soon they met up with the non-fishing wives of visiting fishermen who befriended everyone. And that is how I found out that Horace and his teenage daughter, Olive, were living as a couple! Horace was tight-mouthed and quiet, but Olive, naively, was an open jet mouth. She told anyone anything they wanted to know. Even about coitus with her dad! They soon became the pier's main interest.

One morning as she was deciding how much bait to take out, I moved over closer to her and quietly said, "Olive, I hear that you and your dad are cohabiting in a local apartment. Is that true?"

At first it appeared that she did not understand what was meant by the word "cohabiting."

She stood pronouncing the word over and over until I explained its meaning and then she proudly answered in the affirmative: "Yes, that's true. We just found that place yesterday, which Dad thinks we can afford. It has a cute little kitchen where we can cook our food 'n' all."

"Olive, are you telling me that you and your father sleep together in one bed?"

"Yes. What's wrong with that? We've always slept together."

She was absolutely unashamed and completely unabashed. There was no sense in my telling her that she and her father were living in awful sin. Besides, I was told to stay out of it.

"How long do you intend to stay here in Jax Beach?" I asked, knowing that all vacationers had a tight schedule.

"We don't have any definite plans. Dad says that everything depends on us getting a job. We'll know in a day or so if we'll have work. We applied at the largest restaurant in Mayport, and that guy said it looked pretty good for this weekend. We'll know soon, I guess."

I was astonished at how free and unaffected this girl was. I began to take a deeper notice of this couple. The only way I could describe Olive as being "beautiful" is through her youthfulness. I think being that young is absolutely delightful and gorgeous to everyone's eye, despite her noticeable overbite.

She had exceptionally light-blue eyes, like her dad. Her hair was long, dark, brunette. Olive was about 5' 5" tall, with a splendid figure. She was slim, about 125 pounds. Her clothes were hillbilly awful. She wore mostly cotton shorts and halters, and she seemed to have a couple of slimline cotton skirts which she always wore with a pair of well-worn neutral-colored sandals. Yet the girl seemed to give an impression of loveliness, and drew attention from the opposite sex of all ages.

Light-haired and with light-blue eyes, Horace was not a bad-looking guy. A thin, slight man, he was only an inch or so taller than Olive. I don't remember seeing him wearing shorts; he always arrived wearing long pants and long-sleeved shirts, as if he was afraid of picking up too much sun.

This man found it difficult to look into my eyes. When we were in conversation, he always looked away at something else. I wondered if he understood he was teaching his daughter a sinful way of life.

He must have known that Olive was being criticized and condemned by some of the pier's regular folk. However, he was also teaching Olive to totally disregard what she was hearing.

"Tell them to mind their own damn business," he kept telling her.

When Olive told them exactly that, it created real strife between the fishermen's wives and the wayward father and his daughter.

George Bone and Dick Poole thought Horace was a nutcase and had little more to say about that couple. The pier sold Horace bait and ice and let him go without further discussion.

George advised me to stay out of any befriending. "If a fight breaks out up here on the pier, call the law and let them handle it. The world is full of crackpots like that crazy bird."

I don't remember George having any more to say on this subject.

Arguments started out on the pier and they usually ended before anyone threw a fist or anything else. They would pick up again the next day if Horace and Olive showed up.

A couple of smart-ass young fellows started calling Horace, Mr. Whore's Ass, more in crude fun, I think, than in seriousness. That went nowhere and they quit their annoyances.

A couple of teenage boys pursed their lips together and made sucking sounds at Olive. Olive became annoyed and tormented enough to come to the tackle shop's office to report this harassment.

I was on duty at the time. I picked up the intercom and plugged into the end of the pier where these boys were having their fun. I loudly announced that we were preparing restraints for bad pier behavior that would ban a person from the pier for a long period of time. "So if you fellows want this restraint presented to you, keep up your ugly behavior, and we will see you later as you leave."

Everything went quiet out on the end of the pier.

The loafing wives, however, did a lot of talking and it wasn't long before pure gossip had spread from one end of the pier to the other. They seemed to know when and how the girl was being sexually abused, and confronted her on her activities as if it were the girl's fault.

A couple of fatherly fishermen started to get involved. They were attempting to talk to Horace, without success. As they moved in on Horace, he picked up and went to fish on another part of the pier.

One day Olive came on board with both cheekbones rubbed raw. As the day progressed, her high cheeks grew quite pink and sore-looking. That was the day one older fisherman got so angry, I thought he was going to jump on Horace and beat up on him. But the fisherman merely loudly accused Horace of sexually abusing his daughter, and in a deviate way, because that was the only way she was able to get carpet burns on that part of her face. No one knew what Horace had on his mind because he simply ignored everything pertaining to these accusations.

On his day off, Herschel Sisson, who worked on the *Miss Mayport*, a deep-sea fishing boat, was on the pier seeking customers interested in a deep-sea fishing adventure. He asked me directly if what he heard about Miss Olive was true.

"I'll be damned if I know," I said, "but that seems to be what is going around."

"Feh!" Sisson yelled in disgust. He spat a wad of tobacco juice onto the deck and walked off mumbling to himself.

I was happy to see so many of these ladies taking an interest in Olive. At home, my husband and I agreed that some of what these people preached to the girl would stick and perhaps at a later time and place, work a miracle. Nevertheless, we agreed that first Olive had to remove herself from her father's attachment and grow intellectually.

I learned that she didn't even have a high school diploma or education. She told me she had recently quit in her third year from a county-operated vocational school near Birmingham, Alabama, where she had focused on art. She wasn't trained for anything, such as office work. She certainly didn't appear to be ready to leave home for a career on her own. She loved to draw. While at the pier, using a small penknife she scratched remarkable local scenes on the sides of our large green plastic fishing buckets to show off her talents.

However, she had left school and was dreaming of holding a job, especially because she wanted some new clothes. I remember when I was her age, I too had wanted to hurry out of school to have a job so I could buy some gorgeous new things to wear. For most young adults it is a normal desire to want nice wearing apparel.

Olive had recently left home with her father, and while both were washing dishes and eating well at a busy, large seafood restaurant, a good job was still a question-mark future. She told me she had already applied to join the Army. Her application to the US Army was rejected, and she could not explain why she was refused. I had thought that our country's Army accepted all volunteers, but apparently they have certain requirements which Olive did not fulfill.

Olive seemed to be happy living with her runaway-from-home dad. Several times, she blurted out her love for her father and her concern for his safety.

One day during a terrific thunder and lightning storm, I called out for the fishermen to please come in off the pier for the duration of the storm. While we were bunched up in the mall of the pier, we all learned that a local fishing woman had been killed by lightning at the Guana Lake dam, a few miles down the road on Highway A1A.

Olive was standing against our tackle shop counter. When an explosive thunderbolt lit up the blackened skies, she began to weep, watching her dad make a run for shelter as the dark cloud poured down rain.

"I don't know how I'd survive if I lost my dad," she wailed.

I scooped her up into my arms and gave her a little hug, saying, "It won't be today, Olive, it won't be today."

It wasn't long after this awful storm when the couple arrived at the pier an hour earlier than usual. Horace went into the restaurant and Olive came straight to my counter and began to tear up even before she spoke. I could see she had been crying for some time; her face was swollen and tear-stained. She was full of emotion and urgency.

"Please, Miss Eve, please hide me! Please!"

I was shocked beyond words. "Hide you from what? Or from whom?" I needed to know.

"From my mother and my brother. They are coming here to the pier at ten o'clock." She began to bawl like a dying calf whose life was coming to a terrible end.

I gave her a small glass of Pepsi and insisted she drink at least half of it. Then I began to try to understand what her problem was.

She told me that her mother and brother were coming to have a meeting with her and her dad because they were half of their family. Only, Horace had decided he did not want Olive to participate in the discussion. Then he changed his mind and decided he did not want Olive to see her mother or her sibling. As the hour of the meeting neared, he directed her to approach me and ask to be hidden by letting her into the tackle shop, behind our tackle display board where she could not possibly be seen from any angle on the pier.

As the clock was approaching ten bells, we saw Horace leave the restaurant and head down to the parking lot where he planned to intercept his wife and son. At the same time, I also saw Mr. George Bone heading up the pier's boardwalk ramp. I thought, *He will now find the hysterical Olive inside the tackle shop under my wing, and most certainly I will get bawled out.* I quickly made a decision. I could have rightly refused the girl's request but I chose not to. To avoid any conflict with Mr. Bone, I pushed Olive through the tackle shop and out the side door, on the south side of the pier. There's a bench out there against the south wall, and I told Olive to sit and stay put until her father came back for her.

With customers to take care of, the time went fast. About fifteen or twenty minutes later, Horace was back from his meeting and was looking for Olive. I went out and told her to walk the narrow porch towards the ocean a few feet, turn left at the corner, and she would be rejoined by her father on the pier. The poor girl was still weeping and shaking badly. I told Horace it would be a good idea if he took his daughter to see a doctor because Olive was in a terrible mental condition. They walked off without a word from either of them.

That was the last time I saw the couple. It was plain to see they had moved on. I often wondered how that meeting went and whether or not they went back home to solve their problems.

Then I heard rumors via the pier's grapevine that one of our fishermen's wives, who had left more than a week ago for their home in Kankakee, Illinois, had been in contact with an agency that dealt with incestuous situations. Could she be the reason they disappeared?

For a long time afterward I've hoped and prayed that the comely Miss Olive found herself in good hands and that she at least saw a productive, happy life. She certainly deserved better.

28 – Pier Personalities Thin Out

When you see someone frequently, and especially if they are cordial, nonaggressive people, you tend to feel a deeper warmth towards them. I think it's similar to kinship, sometimes even warmer. Anyway, that's the way it was among the many regular fishing people and me. Because a great many of them were retired and into their later years of life, there was a death now and again to acknowledge. Many of them caused me to grieve. A few affected George Bone's persona enough to make him weep too.

One of the first so-called special people to go on my watch was a darling of a man everyone called "the Chief." George first started calling him that because he was an ex-chief of police of Newark, New Jersey. He was a tall man with a shock of white hair and a large bony face. He made everyone feel good. I could readily understand why he was called "the sweetheart of those who have gone to seed." Never did he pass an elderly person without saying something sunshiny and uplifting. Cancer took him away from us.

...

Mr. Burt McMains from the Caterpillar Company was one whom I cried over. This man was a youngish seventy-year-old who appeared to be a strong, good-looking, healthy man. Burt made no secret of his feelings for me. He not only brought me a freshly made donut every day he came to fish, which was three or four times a week, he also brought me a single flower every Monday morning. And he paid for my lunch every chance he found. At first I didn't know what to make of it because I was not making a play for him. I was happily married. Then I realized he was also happily married, so he was just being friendly in his own way, and I grew to like that special attention.

One day on the pier, around three o'clock in the afternoon, Burt began to bleed from his nose. I took him in behind the tackle shop, out of public view, and I packed the back of his neck with mounds of crushed ice. The bleeding would not stop. After about a half hour, George told me to run him over to the Beaches Hospital, as Burt was losing a lot of blood. At the hospital I sat at his bedside trying to comfort the poor guy because they decided to keep him overnight. They couldn't stop the bleeding. At six o'clock Burt asked me to call his home and tell his wife where he was and why. I did, and Mrs. McMains said she would be at the hospital in ten minutes.

    I lightly kissed Burt on the side of his mouth and said adios until tomorrow. At the door I glanced back to wave goodnight, and I saw his hand on his cheek where I had lightly touched him. The next day at the pier we learned that the Beaches Hospital had taken Burt McMains to Baptist Hospital in downtown Jacksonville. They said they could not stop the bleeding. We never learned if Burt had been treated with Coumadin or some other blood thinner. We never learned why they couldn't stop the bleeding. I'm sad to say this gracious human being never recovered from that strange nosebleed. They held a private funeral. We at the pier really missed Mr. Burt McMains.

…

    A brilliant red-haired egghead from Michigan, Derk Ankka was, like me, a newcomer to Jacksonville Beach. Like me, he fell in love with the art of fishing, and invested in all the necessary paraphernalia. He soon moved into the new high-rise apartment towers at Third Street and Jacksonville Beach Boulevard to be near the pier, which was at Sixth Avenue S. Beyond this, the man was a mystery to us on the pier. He was friendly without becoming friends with anyone. He would say "Hello, how are you," but he didn't stay put to hear your answer. When Virginia, Richard Rogerson's baby-sitter, moved into the same building, we heard that Derk was mysteriously carried out to the hospital one midnight. Then we learned he was taken to the detox center to be dried out. So this handsome man, this retired teacher of mathematics, was hiding his occasional drunkenness! *Okay,* I thought. *He deserved respect from us whom he did not harm. If he is a secret imbiber, let it be.*

One day he was fishing at the end of the pier where the pluggers were hard at work pulling in Spanish mackerel. Someone got a pretty-good-sized one hooked and his rod was doubled over while pulling it up. Derk went over beside the struggling fisherman and bent over the rail, putting his head downward to see the catch. Just then the big fish shook free of the lure and the leaded Sea Hawk sprung up with great force and caught Derk under the chin. The Sea Hawk's top treble hooks were deeply embedded into his lips and the bottom treble hook whipped into his under-chin. The fisherman cut him free from the line, and I drove Derk to the Beaches Hospital to be de-hooked.

From then on, Derk and I became friendlier while fishing on the pier. I learned he had lost his wife, his "best friend and soul mate," about a year before he moved down to Jax Beach, and he was still grieving, he said. He had a beautiful thirty-five-year-old daughter whom I met while she was on a short stay. She was living a gay lifestyle in San Francisco and visited her father at Christmastime.

About a month later, Derk got so inebriated they were unable to save him this time. One of his neighbors found him running up and down the hall in the nude, yelling at the top of his voice that some demon with a machete was chasing after him. He died of acute alcoholism. I was the only one from the pier who went to his funeral service to say goodbye to Derk.

...

John Ballinger was another loner. But he was full of stories whenever he had a few beers. He was not a perpetual drunk, that I noticed, but he was a regular beer drinker. He left his home in Winnebago, Illinois, because he said his sister Sabina cheated him out of a few thousand dollars, his share of their parental holdings. He was also disappointed and "mad as hell" because his one and only daughter was running around with a jobless black man, then married him, and moved in with John. This was totally too much for him, he said. "Hell, no one needs me around here," he stated.

In 1963, John had packed his favorite tools, his underwear, and duds into his pickup and drove off to Jacksonville Beach, Florida. He went to this expanding city knowing of the considerable construction going on here.

Right away he met Mr. Williams, the builder of this pier, who hired him. Next he met George Bone, and together they built the pier's restaurant building. Then they teamed up and built a beautiful ranch-style house for the Williams family. After that, John semiretired and worked only for George Bone on an occasional contract. He preferred to take his retirement and do some fishing. He taught me how to catch flounder, which was his specialty. Never in all the passing years did he contact anyone back home in Illinois.

One day, John's old pickup was stolen with all his tools, about two thousand dollars' worth within it. About two weeks later, he received a phone call from police in Georgia, reporting they had recovered his pickup, and asked when John would come to reclaim it. I remember I was happy to hear what I thought was good news, and I asked when John was planning to go up to reclaim his property. Wily John, however, had called the Georgia police back and asked what, if anything, was still with the vehicle, like his bench saw and other certain power tools. He was advised that the truck had been totally ransacked and very little was found intact. John decided not to make the trip for a wreck worth hardly anything. John turned to full-time fishing and playing pool with his old and sometimes new cronies. The pier became his only interest. He took his meals at the restaurant and hung out all day long.

Not long after the robbery occurred, John had a powerful stroke and wound up at the old veterans hospital in another county.

Jake, one of his pool-playing friends, visited John once a week, and Jake told us that John was completely paralyzed on one side and unable to speak. He suspected that John had decided not to eat; he was getting thinner every time he saw him. Within a couple of days after that report, John died in August of 1980 at the veterans hospital. George Bone and Mr. Williams claimed his body and gave him a burial. George was especially saddened with the loss of this longtime carpentry and pool-playing buddy. Everyone at the pier missed John Ballinger.

…

There was an old guy named Sylvester Branch who lived alone out in the countryside near Palm Valley. We used to call him "I wanna be Mafia." This was because there wasn't a day that went by without his bending our ears with stories about how important he was to the New York area Mafia family.

He said his connection was that he was married to the sister of Antonio Bagliso, and he was often called to help find someone or check something out for the local godfather. We all knew the Mafia people were close-mouthed, and these stories were merely a fixation with Sylvester. He was an aging, mentally disturbed man.

This old guy irritated me so much so that one day I told him to go away and leave me alone. "I am not interested in your Mafia family stuff," I loudly proclaimed. But that didn't stop him from yapping. I was helpless. I couldn't stop him and neither could anyone else. George Bone and Dick Poole would walk away. Ed Davis, however, used to encourage Sylvester's monologues and had a good laugh at him, not with him.

One day someone in his neighborhood punched this poor, sick guy and blackened his eye. He never complained or talked about that. Sometime later, the day came when we heard he had died in his sleep. That meant he wouldn't be coming back to the pier to bug us with his crazy Mafia obsession. Although we were much relieved, I said a little prayer that he would find someone in heaven willing to listen to his annoying discourses. God bless Sylvester.

…

Thank goodness sad things didn't happen too often, but they did happen and I'd be upset for a time after. I remember I was quite new on the job when I met a young woman comforting another Latino lady who was in tears. They were sitting on a bench outside our tackle shop. I thought maybe the crying person was injured by a catfish or jellyfish and maybe needed first aid. So I carefully approached them and asked what the trouble was, and looked to see if I could offer any help.

I was knocked off my keister when the sympathetic lady said, "Thank you. No, my friend must have her sadness. This is the first time she has come back to this beach, where her child disappeared ten years ago."

"What!" I exclaimed. "She lost a child on this beach?" I wanted to understand what she was telling me. "Did the child drown?" I asked softly.

"No one knows for certain," answered the weeping woman's friend. "They never found the boy's body. The child was only five years old. The little boy was digging sand right beside his mother. She had turned her face the other way for a minute to get an even tan, and when she turned back again, the child was gone. He was nowhere around. The little guy was afraid of water and wouldn't have gone near the sea alone. The lifeguards looked for him for a long time. They suspected that a 'chicken hawk,' a pedophile, snatched up the boy and carried him away, along with his little red sand shovel, which was also not found."

I could readily see I was of no help to this cause. Having lost my one and only son in childbirth, I knew she was still grieving over her loss. I went in and got a couple of cold ginger ales and treated them to a refreshing icy drink.

The memory of this tale, however, still haunts me these many years later.

...

As does, also, this tale. A poor family from Georgia's hill country, with three little towheaded boys, used to show up for a week or so of fishing. I have no clue why they stopped coming. Maybe it was because Mr. Poole had warned them there would be no more free fishing. I know George was unhappy that the man and his wife had money to get drunk every night but no money to give George Bone for bait or fishing fees. They begged from everybody for everything. They had no self-respect and pleaded around for their needs. They were even suspected of outright stealing. Gasoline was siphoned from parked cars while they were in town. They were what George and others called "poor white trash."

Their three little blue-eyed, white-headed boys were as cute as could be after their bath in the ocean. They were about five, six, and seven years old. The man worked on Georgia farms picking peaches and digging peanuts—although I often wondered how the father was able to work with only one good hand. His right hand was missing at the wrist. He told George he had lost it "in a fight with a goddamn n— who chopped it off."

The wife was a big, messy-looking woman, but strong in appearance. She used rough language with her boys and husband. The husband was on the short and skinny side, with light-blond hair and a baby face. They apparently slept on the beach, and parked their decrepit jalopy of a car as close to the public beach as possible. They slept in the car when it rained. When I last saw them, a terrible thing had happened.

They had just arrived at Jacksonville Beach and were about to park in their favorite area near the public boardwalk and the Ferris wheel, where the amusements were located. They had to wait for a parking place to open, so they circled the block, waiting and watching. The seven-year-old asked to be let out of the car. He wanted to run down to the ocean's edge and get his feet wet. They let him go and then found a place to park.

The next thing they knew, the mother told us, they saw their kid staggering and struggling to walk towards them. Within those few intervening minutes, the seven-year-old boy had been raped and sodomized among the giant rocks on his way back from the water. He was taken to the Beaches Hospital with a torn and bleeding rectum. *My God,* I thought, *what a horrible thing to happen to a poor little boy!* He suffered from complications following that experience and was a long time in the hospital.

At about this same time I learned that parents had to watch out for their little boys as much as, or more so, than their daughters because a TV report by the Phil Donahue program described a nationwide Man-Boy Society whose philosophy was that parents should understand that their little boys should be allowed to have sex with strangers. I had a preschool grandson at that time and I began to worry about his safety whenever they came to visit us in Jax Beach. I never saw that family from Georgia again and have wondered if that little boy ever fully recovered from his ordeal. I prayed that he did.

...

No matter what age, children should be watched at all times by someone in charge. My case in point would be the son of Robert and Marilyn Muggry, who drowned in full view of his distracted mother on the pier. Robert Jr. was ten years of age and able to take good care of himself, and often helped his handicapped sister with her schoolbags and stuff. He was a strong boy, a good swimmer, and was not a careless type. But he drowned in a rip current, to our horror and disbelief.

The summer heat in Jacksonville Beach can be oppressive unless one is in the water, and then it is quite enjoyable. The beaches get packed with people whenever the temperature climbs to eighty degrees or more. The ocean's currents in this part of the Atlantic Ocean are caused by the trade winds. If the wind is from the south, the beach currents move northward; if they are from the north or the northeast, the current moves towards the south. In the spring and summer the winds are often from northeast storms. And if there are two or three days of intense, stormy northeast wind, the waves grow larger and the rip currents become stronger. The waves on the beach get churned into frothy whiteness and knock grown people head over heels.

These same currents occur in August, September, and October, when the winds develop from the direction of Africa. We get some very strong winds along with the hurricane season. The seas at this beach reach nine and ten feet tall, and the rip currents are only for experienced surfers and their boards. On such dangerous days, the lifeguards discourage people from entering the water because of the rip currents. The lifeguards are sometimes very busy rescuing people from the angry surf.

The worst rip currents are caused mostly at full tide, when the high seas keep throwing water up on the beach. And when those waters thrown up on the shore recede and start to find their way back out to sea again, the rip tide catches and carries people out with its force.

Mrs. Muggry was up on the pier fishing with her new heartthrob when she heard the guards frantically whistling and saw them running around like crazy, pulling people back to safety that day.

Then she saw the rescue ambulance come to carry someone off to the hospital. That's when she decided she had better run down and check on her two children. Shockingly, she discovered her twelve-year-old daughter was receiving first aid, and it was her young son, Robert, who went off with the rescue wagon. He was pronounced dead on arrival.

A good surfer had rescued the daughter and brought her in on his board, but when the surfer went back for Robert, the boy was found beneath the water, unable to fight his way back through the heavy rip current.

It was a terribly sad day for many of us who were on the pier and witnessed this tragedy.

…

The day Richard Rogerson died was not only grievous and sorrowful, but completely unexpected. At the pier, he was the main counterbalancing personality whom nearly everybody consulted whenever a serious problem arose, and he acted as a real honest-to-goodness friend to most of us.

Only the day before, he had knocked on my kitchen window and asked if I could please accompany him to the Orchard Park Dog Races. He was the only one who came knocking on my window rather than on my door. Nearing six months since his open-heart surgery, he said he never felt better in his life. However, he had promised his wife, Muriel, that he would not drive out of town alone. It was getting on towards afternoon racing time, so he wanted my help.

He said he was fed up with cabin fever, tired as heck of staying home, and felt a need to go to the track because he felt luck falling his way. I had never been to any Florida dog track.

I told him, "Richard, I would be glad to go with you, but I don't gamble, so wouldn't you want to ask someone else to accompany you?"

Richard hemmed and hawed and said, "No, Eve, everyone was working and since you are my nearest neighbor, and since Linwood is on the road this week, and since it's your day off, I thought you might be available."

He looked into my eyes so imploringly that I changed my mind and agreed to go along.

On this clear, shiny day, Richard drove unerringly. We chatted about our kids and families. He had two boys in college by his first wife, and wanted to help them get started in life. He now had a brand-new baby boy with his pretty new wife, Muriel. He couldn't say enough about Michael and could hardly wait to take him fishing.

When we got to the race track, I told Richard not to pay any attention to me, to study his racing form as if I weren't there, and I wished him good luck on his betting. I then went down to the paddock to look the dogs over, and that's where I stayed most of the afternoon.

Greyhounds are an interesting animal and have been around since early Egypt, when the pharaohs preferred them above all other breeds of the time. The usual colors of these middle-weight dogs are fawn, white, black, brindle, and gray and white with patches. I watched as they amicably nuzzled one another, while others were busy smelling both ends of neighbors, and a few showed mild aggressions while on this pre-race display in the paddock.

For the sixth or seventh race, out came a group of greyhounds with one big, solid gray dog standing a mile taller than all the rest. She caught my eye and I watched in great surprise when she squatted to urinate. My goodness sakes! That dog was full of water! Her puddle began to run down and on and on and on it flowed. I never saw any other dog pee so much water. It occurred to me that this dog would now be so much lighter that it would be able to fly over the tops of all the others. I decided I'd tell Richard about my observation and advise him to put some money on that big gray dog. I hurried to find Richard.

"No, no," he hollered back. "I know that dog's owner and he said Big Gray was through racing. They had already retired Big Gray and only brought her out today to fill a vacancy in the pack. No, Eve, that dog's career as a racer is over," Richard said with finality.

I decided I had to put some money where my mouth was and bet on the Big Gray! I knew I was low on cash and looked within my purse to see what I had. Luckily I had a couple of dollars and some change, and so I ran for the betting window with my two dollars in hand. I placed the bet just under the bell, which rang, closing down all betting windows! The race began, and I saw Big Gray loping along. As soon as she saw the rabbit she flew into high gear. She passed the whole pack, easily winning the race. I had proven my theory, and the track paid me fifty bucks!

Richard said, "I'll be damned." He said that because he had lost every race he had picked and was out the fifty dollars he had brought.

By nine o'clock next morning George and Ann and Mr. Poole, Ed Davis, and everybody at the restaurant had heard of my lucky win and the story of how I came to make the bet. George, who frequented the track more than anyone else there, said he had never been down to the paddocks; it had never occurred to him to go there. "It was her beginner's luck," he said, to explain my win.

....

Later that day Richard went for one of his several daily walks on the beach, and that is where an athletic runner found him lying in the sand, dead to this world. The young lady said she at first thought the figure ahead was a log thrown up by the last high tide, but when she neared the darkly clad object, she saw it was a human being lying prone. She struggled to turn him over, she said, to see what had happened, and found he was not breathing. She ran up to Ocean 14, the nearest building, and placed a call to 911.

So we all went to the First Christian Church of the Beaches on Neptune Beach and cried together over Richard's passing. Richard was only fifty-one years old. George was especially afflicted with sorrow and cried audibly. I decided to go sit beside him and touch his hand, which seemed to help quiet his uncontrolled feelings. I knew George was a good man, and all that tough talk he was known for was to hide his real perceptivity, and this occasion proved that to be so.

I told Muriel I was sorry I had not accepted Richard's invitation to eat supper hamburgers with his family after the races the previous night, because "I could have gained another hour or so in his charming company." She understood, I know. Little Michael was a toddler. It would be some time before he would understand what all the crying and blowing of noses was about. I looked around at the people crowded into the small church, and up front to the left I saw Richard's older sons and his former wife. They looked vanquished and forlorn from deep sorrow.

What can one say of a loved one's death? What was living is no longer living, and the emptiness now created denies access to the mysteries of death. Saddened by death's extent and silenced by its stillness, they were left to mourn; for without mourning the loss is unbearable. And they all looked unto themselves for the final secret and for the final understanding.

Sudiev (Good-bye), Richard. It was good to know you.

29 – Marilyn's Homeless Story

The day that Marilyn Spevack arrived at the pier was something else. A lot of difficult people crossed our paths on the pier, but Marilyn was a special entity. First of all, she never fished for even one day, but she was constantly on the pier and for a long time. The visiting fishermen's wives who hung around the pier got tired of her long before we did.

It all happened because of one of our older employees, a man we called Captain Ernie. Like George Bone, Ernie was not a licensed captain at all, yet we thought he too deserved the title. He was a sentimental individual who saw a likeness of his own daughter in Marilyn and, so, extended a special friendliness towards her. He was responsible for her long visit; after he heard her story the morning after her first night's stay, he allowed her to stay over again and again and again and again.

With permission from the boss, he made sure the rest of the employees agreed to follow his example. Of course the pier's staff agreed to his case in point and we all treated Marilyn with dignity and respect. That wasn't difficult to do.

Marilyn had come up on the pier one night with the help and advice of a total stranger who happened to walk upon a commotion between a man and a woman on the beach. The night walker paused in his exercising and saw a serious altercation going on between a man who was sexually forcing himself upon a woman lying on a dark blanket and crying out for help. This good person pulled out his cell phone and called 911. A cruiser happened to be parked a few hundred feet north of the pier, in the area we called the "nocturnal battle zone." Two policemen responded and were on top of things in no time and removed the surprised molester.

After the squad car left with the masher, the walking man tried to calm the lady in distress. He noticed that this person was well dressed and had an expensive Latin-American cloak and beach bag which was being trampled on, so he decided this lady looked extremely decent and he didn't feel right leaving her unattended after such a shocking intrusion. The good Samaritan then told her she looked to be a responsible person, and suggested she might want to consider camping up on the pier because there were always a few people around who would help keep her safe throughout the night, better than down there on the sand. She agreed, and he helped carry her stuff up on the pier, where she settled down for the night on a long bench high over the thrashing Atlantic Ocean.

Marilyn was a spectacular-looking Polish American woman, displaying a well-built five-foot-six-inch frame and natural, thick blond hair. She wore a sassy Sassoon haircut dipping lower on one side, and when she looked at you, one could not resist marveling over her sparkling blue eyes. On first notice she had a quiet, aristocratic manner about her. With a second observation one could readily see she had a natural talent for worming her way into one's heartstrings, making everyone want to help her in any way they could. I thought this Spevack woman was a close resemblance to Zsa Zsa Gabor of Hollywood fame. In fact, at first I thought it was Zsa Zsa who had come to our pier.

Recently back from South America, Marilyn wore only Columbian-made stuff, which made her stand out from our locals. In the morning she prepared for the beach by wearing a well-cut black bathing suit and a large, wide-brimmed, black felt sombrero-type hat that always accompanied her while in the sun. A gaily flowered mid-calf wrap, cadmium yellow on a field of azure blue, covered her lovely long legs when off the beach. Later in the day she always wore one of her two stunning black cotton sundresses, with simple leather black sandals on her well-kept dainty feet. It was amazing to me how she was able to keep her things looking so fresh and new in appearance, the way she lived out of a tote bag. Marilyn was not a show-off, but everything she put on was pleasing to the eye of the beholder.

Though not an overly friendly person, Marilyn acted pleasantly towards everyone. However, she shunned most of the fishermen's wives, who tried their damnedest to befriend her. She probably sensed they were trying to find out more about her background so they could chatter away, but Marilyn was never cold to them, just extra careful. A woman from Kankakee, Illinois, was especially striving to befriend Marilyn by bringing her tasty things like a cream puff or a bear claw from the Publix bakery. Marilyn always thanked her sweetly, and once I watched her pinch a tiny piece from the cake and refuse the rest on grounds that she was dieting. I often wondered what the plumpish lady from Kankakee thought at times like that. As far as I could see, none of those visiting women ever sat and chatted with Marilyn for more than a second. I could tell they were curious as heck about this person who hung about the pier as long as she did. Marilyn's habit was to say "Good morning!" as pleasantly as she could to everyone and proceed on her way as if she had a great deal on her mind.

The fishermen all had pleasant looks on their faces whenever they were in Marilyn's presence, but never engaged her in conversation, that I knew of. They may have asked Captain Ernie about her, and only God knows what, if anything, he had to say.

Marilyn seemed to like me and spent a lot of time in my company. One Wednesday evening I invited her to Sonny's Bar-B-Q when they had their nickel-beer-nights, and she accepted. It turned out to be an especially pleasant evening. It was affordable and, henceforth, I felt good being able to treat her to this weekly supper-party. Sometimes we were four, five, or even six whenever we were joined by friends or my family members. My people liked her and thought she was interesting. Dinner with Marilyn became a weekly habit and I looked forward to it.

I told Marilyn she could have ribs or chicken or anything she wanted from the menu. Most of the time she ordered the same as I did. My favorite Wednesday supper was a large pork barbecue on a bun, along with a bowl of baked beans and coleslaw. The barbecue was served with a generous scoop of french fries. With the three allowed nickel-beers, we were stuffed. Sometimes Marilyn only went for the salad bar, but she never refused the beer. We had fun times, like discussing places we'd been in this wide world and discovering we were both well traveled. We ate and laughed away the entire hour in sheer pleasure.

One could not imagine what I picked up during our dinner dates. Surprisingly, I learned that this homeless person had a doctorate degree in medical psychiatry and she'd had a flourishing clinic in

Plantation, Florida. Recently she had to close down because she got so sick she was unable to get to her office daily.

"When you can no longer pay your rent, it is time to close," she sadly explained.

"Marilyn, what the heck is wrong with you?" I boldly asked. "You look perfectly healthy to me."

"I'm not," she confessed softly. "In layman's terminology, I am a complicated bipolar patient, bordering, I'm told, on schizophrenia. I am on daily medication, or I would become terribly depressed and uncontrollable when these episodes come over me."

"Oh, for goodness sakes," I said, "what happens if you can't afford to buy your medication or simply forget to take it?" I asked this second question in empathy because I am one who rarely remembers to take occasional medication.

"My dear, you don't want to know." Marilyn looked straight into my eyes and acknowledged her disease in this way: "I become so bad I'm not fit to be around civilized people."

That was the first time I saw tears fall from Marilyn's limpid eyes.

"Oh, no," I whispered. "Do you have any close kin who understand your problem? Where could you go in an emergency?" I was thinking of the oncoming cool weather when summer cotton sundresses would no longer be enough around the Jacksonville area.

"My mother and sister live in Pennsylvania, just outside of Philadelphia, but they are both crazier than I am. I can't get along with either of them. Neither would be of any help to me. Even my shrink has told me this." She confided this without hesitation.

I felt myself shiver. I couldn't imagine having those same thoughts about my mother and sister. I felt even more sorrowfully towards Marilyn. I thought for sure this person must know what mental hell must be like, and I teared up too.

"What brings these episodes on? You seem so normal to me. I can hardly believe what you are telling me, Marilyn."

"Please believe me, Eve. Usually I go off into a world of my own, following a deep disappointment or some shocking news. This last episode came over me right after my sweet husband of eight and a half years surprised me by asking for an immediate divorce so that he could go back to Miami to marry his much younger, pregnant secretary."

"Oh, what a rat!" I exclaimed in shocked horror. But I was not wordless. "Were you unhappily married?"

"No," she quickly answered. "No, we were both happy, for all I knew. He was a fellow doctor, and we were both thirty-one when we married. We were joyful with our professions and loved to travel on our vacation time. This past year we went to Colombia, South America, to visit some old college friends. This is where I noticed Danny was making frequent calls back to his Miami office. Nonchalantly, I asked if he had an emergency he was worried about, and that is when he hit me with the necessity of getting an immediate divorce.

"There was no discussion. He packed up and left to go back to Miami. It was more than I could understand. Confused, I joined some other travelers to snort some cocaine, which was cheap, and it made me feel a lot better. But then I woke up one morning and I was well into the throes of a bipolar episode. Our Bogotá friends saw me rant and cuss and carry on, and convinced me to return to the States. Two friends brought me back and we checked in with a special shrink located at the Mayo Clinic in Jacksonville. They made the arrangements and brought me here. I was sleeping on the beach because I can't afford a hotel as yet. But according to my doctor, I am getting better every passing day. And soon I will be getting more alimony support from Danny, he assures me.

"I miss Danny. I had noticed our lovemaking had been getting sparse, but I thought it was normal as our lives got busier. Still, I loved it so when he used to put his warm and tender body close to mine ... sleep was always so comforting. Now all I get is a cold stipend in parting. It's hardly enough to get by on. That's the reason why I live like I do. If I can live on the beach without cost, I can make do anywhere, so I had thought. Everything was fine until that no-good bum attacked me.

"But Captain Ernie and the people on the pier are empathetic souls, and I appreciate what they have done for me. I hope to repay them somehow, someday."

"I've been here on the pier for a few years," I said, "and I have never seen this happen before." I had to tell her the truth as I saw it.

Marilyn usually woke up about 6:00 a.m., but turned over and slept another hour or two before she actually started to move around. She would put on her sexy bathing suit and skirt, have breakfast, and then down to the beach for the rest of the day she'd go. She now owned a large yellow bedsheet someone contributed to her welfare and this she'd spread out in the sun near the shade of the pier's entrance boardwalk which she could use as a shelter during the heat of the day. She was careful not to sunburn her body. She read *The New Yorker* magazine incessantly and dozed off when her eyes tired.

At around two o'clock the hot dog caddie that was usually found outside the front door of Home Depot made a swing-by on the beach, and Marilyn would have a doggie dressed with sauerkraut and mustard. That is all she ate, until seven or eight o'clock at night. She then warmed up a can of Campbell's Mushroom or Chicken Soup for her supper. At first she asked permission to use the tackle shop's microwave oven to warm her food. But soon she began to take it for granted it was okay to use anything in the shop. If she was aware of the protest silently beginning to be exhibited by the fishermen's wives, she ignored it. I didn't say a word about it to anyone, but I noticed the envy and resentment mounting in their less-than-cordial remarks. I marveled at the way Marilyn was able to completely evade this.

I also know it is a frightful thing for a forty-year-old woman to be away from a source of warm water for extended periods. Especially during the week of the menstrual period when female hygiene needs special attention. However, Marilyn knew how to keep herself as fresh as a flowering specimen, with frequent sponge baths whenever the salty ocean was too rough or otherwise unfit to enter. She said she'd often used the ladies' room at the public library where they had a good supply of large paper towels. She would soap up her top half and sponge off, and then do the bottom half and emerge as a sweet-smelling individual.

Now that she lived on the pier, so to speak, she discovered the handy garden hose lying coiled on the deck just outside the tackle shop, which she made good use of. On certain days she arose early, before anyone was about, and she dragged that hose into the pier's outside toilet shed behind the tackle shop. There she removed her clothing and gave herself a good, thorough, soapy bath. She was never without soap. I knew that the lady from Kankakee used to gift her sachets and perfumed soaps.

Marilyn was street smart enough to know how to avoid getting dry skin and those annoying itchy scales and body lice which many homeless people are plagued with. It was a wonder to many, to see how well she functioned without what is called "a real home."

After a couple of months alone, Marilyn found a "significant other" and she instantly became extremely happy. Often, other homeless people showed up at the pier. But most were on their way to other places and weren't here in public view too long. Captain Ernie used to call them "roosters" and often pointed them out to me.

"Here's a new rooster in town," he'd say as he and I watched a fellow crawl under the boardwalk after sundown, scouting around for a place to drop for the night. Sometimes they came up on the pier looking for a handout. Ed Davis never turned a hungry person down, but most of the others ignored people like that.

Otto Morman was homeless because he and his wife had a serious, harsh spat and in the heat of the battle she kicked him out. He came to Jacksonville Beach to fish and to think things out in his life, as he explained. Otto wasn't broke. He drove a new Chevy pickup truck and had several high-priced fishing sticks. He dressed well and wore an expensive Accutron watch. His name and address on the panel of his truck door read: "Licensed Contractor, Raleigh, North Carolina." This meant he could do carpentry work anywhere, anytime, and have a good income.

Otto located himself in a comfortable rooming house near the pier, and he fished every day. He ate his meals at the pier, and whenever he had a decent catch he paid the cook to prepare it for him. Whenever Ed Davis was on duty as the chef, he never charged anyone for deep-frying their catch. But this loner didn't mind paying and often left a sizable tip.

Otto liked to share his splendid seafood. I once noticed that he invited George Winterling, the area's popular climatologist who often dined alone on the pier. The two men amicably shared a Florida pompano and sat chatting for a long time afterward.

One day Otto invited Marilyn to share his speckled trout and she accepted. The two of them enjoyed the camaraderie of the feast. That was how it started. Otto then frequently looked for Marilyn's company and pretty soon they were dining daily at the pier, and elsewhere.

Otto escorted Marilyn to the movies and the zoo. Soon they began to take overnight trips to Savannah, Atlanta, and Birmingham, Alabama. After about a month of romancing, it was conceded that they were now mutually trading body fluids. And Marilyn was visibly ecstatic with joyful happiness. She felt wanted and loved. She was head over tin cups in love!

She began to speak of marriage to the handsome, sinewy man from North Carolina. All seemed to be going well for both of them until one day he didn't show up at the pier. Marilyn was beside herself, believing Otto had become ill from eating too many raw oysters. She envisioned him lying on the floor in excruciating pain, unable to phone or get help. She decided to go to his rooming house to help him.

There she discovered his digs vacated and all his stuff gone. He had left town without any sort of farewell. Right away Marilyn knew he had returned to his wife, because he was in daily contact with his little boy, his only child. He had left without a word after he had professed love to her, and because she believed him and this man meant so much to her, Marilyn collapsed on the spot.

Another scene evolved at the pier. Captain Ernie tried to console her with friendly words of wisdom, but Marilyn immediately became bitter towards him and everyone in sight. She became boisterous and screamed obscenities as loudly as she could.

"No, no, I can't believe it, I can't believe it, I won't believe it," she shouted over and over in a singsong manner. Then it seemed like she was beginning to believe something as she started screaming repeatedly, "Predator! Predator! Fucking predator!"

Marilyn's distress overpowered her dignity as she ranted like a fishwife. "That son-of-a-bitch predator!" she kept yelling so that the whole world would hear and know she was mad as a hornet. "That no-good, son-of-bitch-predator, that bastard predator!"

Her rants were getting progressively louder by the minute. No one was able to quiet her down; she ignored everybody who tried to console her. It was as if she didn't know her old friends who tried to comfort her.

By the second hour of hearing her rage, Captain Ernie began to worry what could happen, considering her bipolar condition. Ernie reckoned that when she was in her crazy cycle she might accuse him of molesting her, and it would be her word against his. He became afraid of her and of possible trouble. Captain Ernie began to worry.

The wives of the fishermen showed no sympathy or warmth towards Marilyn's situation. They immediately became more vocal. One of them faced her early on and loudly proclaimed: "That's what happens sometimes, Marilyn, when one messes around with a married man."

Another wife said the same thing, only more strongly: "What can you expect when you tangle with a married man? If I were you, I'd shut the hell up!"

They empathized with Otto as they visualized a happy reunion taking place in a North Carolina home, and they actually told Marilyn she was an absolute nut to get herself involved like that. I never heard anyone call Otto Morman a cad.

As poor Marilyn railed on and on, Captain Ernie gave the situation careful consideration and decided to call the police about this unfortunate matter. He had had enough of Marilyn.

The police came right away and they easily saw what was bothering Ernie: Marilyn was hard into her bipolar episode. During the heat of her new affair with Otto she had neglected to take her medications on time, and missed several appointments with her doctor, to boot.

The first policeman came right out and said, "Hello, Marilyn. We understand that you were jilted by a man from North Carolina, and you must be feeling badly over it, right?"

They immediately saw non-normal behavior by what followed.

Marilyn screamed, "That no-good son-of-a-bitch mother-fucker-predator-bastard should have his *cojones* shot off!"

That's how she began to explain her distressing thoughts to the officer's question. The eyes of the policemen enlarged with shock and understanding. That was all they had to hear to be convinced that the lady was quite sick. She kept muttering the same thing over and over.

"Come on, Marilyn," the other policeman said. "Let's get your things packed so that we can get you squared away."

The two young officers did most of the gathering together of her sparse property which had been standing in corners of the tackle shop. They wrapped everything together in her Colombian serape and took her away.

That was the last time any of us ever saw Marilyn Spevack. We were told she had been taken to the hospital. She never again called or visited us at the pier. Of course Captain Ernie and the rest us hoped Marilyn was cured of the vulgar devils that ransacked her head, and is able to partake a comfortable life wherever she is.

I missed Marilyn for a long, long time.

ل

30 – The Handsome Visitor Was a Dangerous Felon

The days beginning in late autumn when we were not so busy, we had time to notice things that did not ordinarily concern us at the tackle shop counter. Thus we noticed people who came up on the pier but did not pay to walk the length of the pier or to fish. The big garage-type doors on both sides were closed down because of the cooler weather, and we admitted paying customers through the small pier doorways. The fee collection for walking was steady throughout the entire day. However, people sometimes milled around in the center hallway without further interest in going outside on the pier. Sometimes quite a bit of the day's income came from walkers, so we stood ready to greet them when they approached our tackle shop counter.

People had many reasons why they paid or didn't pay to walk out onto Bone's Pier. Some were interested to see what kinds of fish were being caught. Some thought they were closer to God out there and these would sit and linger to commune with Him in serious prayer.

Others were interested in watching the rolling Atlantic Ocean, many for the very first time in their lives. Still others were looking for the best angle to communicate with the shorebirds of the moment; and many found outstanding photographs to take back home. Some folks didn't even look out of the window at the ocean and beyond, heading straight for the restaurant to buy a beer or a drink of choice and returning to the beach sand with cup in hand.

One slow morning I watched a handsome young man come sauntering up the entrance ramp. He immediately made me think of the preppy young lawyer I used to work with back in Albany, New York, when I was in the real estate business. This man was dressed in stylish gray slacks and a well-fitting long-sleeved shirt, much like our lawyers used to wear. I knew he was not going to fish because he was without any type of fishing rod or gear. *Here comes a walker,* I thought, but I was wrong. That fellow didn't even look my way as he headed for the restaurant, where he sat down to eat breakfast. He came again at eight o'clock the next morning, and the next, and the next. He was around for at least a week or ten days, never showing any interest in our fishing pier.

One day I shouted out, "Good morning to you!" just before he opened the door to enter the restaurant. Charmingly, he returned my smile and greeting as he went in for his coffee, and the ice between us was broken. *Ah-ha,* I thought, *there is an interesting-looking chap. I'd bet he is a new lawyer in this growing town.*

The following morning at eight o'clock, this young man came and seated himself in the same chair nearest to the front counter, with his back to the rear of the room. He always sat there, nearest the restaurant's porch door and watched the ocean in complete privacy during his breakfast. That particular morning I went into the restaurant for my cup of hot grits and as I was leaving to get back to my post I stopped beside his table to say hello. He smiled with a gracious nod and wished me a "Good morning."

I introduced myself and asked for his name. He said it was "Chris." Then, like I had done with most tourists, I asked where he was from, taking for granted that he was not from Jacksonville Beach. To this question he reacted in a peculiar manner. His body noticeably stiffened and seemed to shrink and his facial muscles instantaneously took on a strange frown. Just then, the tackle shop's phone began to ring and I excused myself.

On my way back to my station I thought, *My goodness, that fellow can shrivel up like a snake.* Earlier in the week I had stepped out of my back door at home and found an attractive charcoal-gray and white striped snake on my patio, and as I hovered above, appraising it, the snake stopped moving and plainly shrank itself in size. That was how this impressive stranger affected me; his response to my innocent question made me think back to that moment with the snake. I began to wonder about him. It was plain to see that he had either forgotten where he was from or had to think of a good answer to my inquiry. But I chose to run off rather than wait for an answer. I didn't want to be told it was none of my business, which it wasn't.

Later in the afternoon that very same day I was sitting out in my backyard on Thirteenth Avenue S. and Second Street, when I saw this

"Chris" on Second Street walking towards my corner. *Maybe I'll engage him in another conversation and learn where he's from,* I thought. But he saw me and veered away, crossing the street towards the south and clearly avoiding any contact with me. Now I wondered about him even more. I got up from my chaise lounge and went out to the edge of Second Street to see where he was going. He disappeared into the house on the northwest corner, at the end of Second Street at Sixteenth Avenue S., across from the tennis courts. As far as I know, he never came back to the pier and I never saw him again, and I forgot about him.

Months went by, and then one day a big lead story with a large photograph in the center of page one appeared in the *Florida Times-Union*, announcing the capture of the "most wanted" Ted Bundy, the monster-like culprit who had tortured and murdered several Florida State University students in Tallahassee, and who had raped and killed twelve-year-old Kimberly Leach, a junior high school student in Lake City, Florida!

Holy smokes! I thought. This photo was clearly that of the handsome "Chris" whom I had met earlier in the year on Bone's Pier! I wondered if anyone else remembered him.

I ran into the restaurant with the picture and pushed it in front of Jake Brown as I said, "Jake, look who you've cooked breakfast for!"

"I'll be damned!" was all I heard after he read the first couple of lines.

Clearly in shock, Jake, the Arty one, turned and proceeded to gather things from one of his tables. He said nothing more, but I could see that he, too, remembered the personable visitor to our pier.

After I studied the story again it turned out that "Chris" was already on the lam when he was at our pier. He had committed numerous horrendous murders in the far West. He had escaped from a county jailhouse in the Northwest and had found his way south to Northeast Florida with the help of stolen vehicles. Apparently he was taking it easy here in Jacksonville Beach, gaining back his strength before he went on his new killing spree. The authorities said he had killed thirty-five and possibly more times, and believed he may have killed as many as one hundred times or more. He was caught in a stolen car.

Born the same year as my oldest child, Theodore Robert "Ted" Bundy, born Theodore Robert Cowell on November 24, 1946, in Burlington, Vermont, was tried and convicted and given the penalty of death in Florida. He was executed at the Florida State Prison in Starke, on January 24, 1989, at the age of forty-two.

This account proves how diverse the pier's visitors were. We had all types of people come through. I thought it was important enough to include here, especially for the benefit of my two young nieces, Christine and Stacy, to show how innocently one can find themselves in the company of a human killing machine.

I can still see this handsome young man withdraw and shrink in size, just like a snake.

31 – Apparently the Perfect Crime

As I look at my "back then" pictures, I hear a thousand words from every scene. The sunrise of early spring was indescribably beautiful. The heartfelt greetings from those whom I met then are in the same category.

Jack, the retired ex-chief of the Newark Police Department, cheered everyone he came across. Jersey Joe once was a swarthy interstate truck driver, and another of those fine early people ready to help someone haul up a sizeable black drum fish. Catfish Miller, a superb fisherman, brought his two handsome teenage sons on Saturday mornings, and they always went home with fish caught early. I shall never forget Catfish because he was generous enough to repair an ancient antique art supply box that was accidentally crushed in my garage. Mr. A. Rollins, an executive with a leading Chicago meat packing company, always brought good news. And my all-time favorite early man was Burt McMains, retired executive from Caterpillar Tractor Company, who used to bring me freshly made jelly donuts. Mmm-mmm, good! I salivate even now with this old memory.

...

One fine crisp April morning, Annie Huckabee and I agreed that because of the full moon that day, it was going to be an exceptionally good day, or a very bad day for people fishing with dead bait. As it turned out, the bluefish began biting early and were around for most of the day. They were caught mostly on dead cut mullet. There was a crisp east wind blowing about twelve to fifteen knots per hour, churning up the white surf to about six or seven feet, which lasted all day long.

The parade of early folks was in mid-gear when a man stepped up to pay his twenty-five-cent walking fee. "Thank you very much," I said with my morning smile. As I automatically stamped his left hand I noticed he was carrying a rather large package in the other hand. That package was heavily wrapped up with masking tape. I think it was the multi rounds of tape on that package that drew my attention to it more than anything else. The package would hold a bushel, but was rectangular in shape.

"What do you have in that package?" I asked with the same smile.

"Oh, I just have some real goodies here," said the young man in a loud, annoyed type of voice, and out he went.

Next in line was Mr. Walter Yonsick.

"Walter," I said, "please keep an eye on that fellow ahead of you and see what he is up to."

"Why?" asked the older one. "Why should I keep an eye on that fellow?"

"Because we don't know what is in his wrapped-up box, do we? He could have his dead dog, or the ashes of his mother, but he could also be carrying something else with intent to harm us all ...."

Walter took off without further comment. It seems that I had taken care of one or two customers when Walter was back, leaning over my counter, saying, "There he goes, Eve!" He was pointing to the back of that young man, now leaving the pier empty handed. "He slung his package out into the ocean, turned around, and left," Walter reported, and he left to go out fishing.

That's all there was to that strange walker. He was noticed by several people out on the end of the pier and they too wondered what he had in the secured package which he threw into the ocean "with such force, as if with a vengeance," Annie Huckabee said. "That young man looked angrily about as if he were quite disturbed," she added. Then I too remembered thinking he sounded disturbed when he went through and told me he had "some real goodies" in his box.

I'd say he was just under six feet tall, a husky, half-bearded fellow wearing a gray-and-tan long-sleeved plaid shirt and an Australian-style leather hat. I had never seen him before, and did not see him after that day.

When George came in about eight the next morning I thought I would tell him this peculiar story and see what he made of it. But George was used to seeing people come to dump trash and other illegal stuff from his pier and gave it no consideration at all.

"He probably was parting with his dead pet," George said, and then dismissed the thought.

It so happened that when I opened the door to the south side of the tackle shop and looked down on the screaming birds on the beach sands below, my eyes caught sight of a long stretch of cardboard with a big bunch of tangled yellow masking tape hanging on to it, and I recognized it to be the parcel we were just talking about.

"Look, George," I said with some surprise in my voice, "there is that guy's package, which the surf washed straight back to shore last night."

"Go down and take a look around," George said. "I know you won't feel right until you have a look there."

I went down among those early-morning, squawking, screaming gulls and, with a small piece of driftwood, I spread out the corners of the original cardboard box that was still attached to the massive amount of masking tape, and my eyes popped out!

There in the seams of the box I rolled out a pair of men's jockey shorts, small to medium in size. This underwear was originally stark white, I could tell, but now the crotch was quite rust-colored and blotchy; it was discolored badly. Every woman knows how bloody white underwear can look if not put through a wash with bleach. Then I saw the fine line of the cut made by stabbing which had taken place right beside the crotch seam. There was not another thing in this broken package, and nothing on the beach either; only the pack of screaming gulls may have witnessed more.

I stood up and saw George Bone looking down on me. To show my horror I clutched my head and pointed down at the sandy mess beside me. George yelled for me to bring the stuff up to the tackle shop.

Poole was now there, and so were a couple of the early people. All who saw the evidence were convinced that a horrific stabbing crime had been committed and said the police should be notified at once. A middle-aged detective showed up two hours later. After staring down at the three-inch stab cut in the blood-soaked jockey shorts and the sandy box and masking tape, he silently shook his head and told us absolutely nothing. He loaded it all up in a clean garbage bag from the pier's supply and took it with him. He never asked any questions or wrote anything down. None of us ever heard anything more about the stab-marked, blood-soaked underwear, or about the individual who once wore them.

I think I was one of about six or seven people who briefly saw the face of the man who may have committed the perfect crime.

32 – The Bank Robbery

Back in 1972 there was a community bank located on First Street in the business district, along with a five-and-ten cent store and a village theatre. One morning, this bank was robbed, and a number of us saw the yegg get caught on the pier. It seems the thief had given his plan much thought; however, he got nabbed quite early on. I think the name of the bank was the Ocean State Bank and it happened to be where we kept our meager savings, so we were happy the bandit didn't get away. He was a fisherman, so I doubt that he was all bad. It seems that the young man had first been to the pier to fish, then, as a second thought, got the idea to go rob our bank.

I had just reported to work. George Bone was there talking to Mr. Poole. It was a run-of-the-mill type of day with mostly the same early fishermen trying to catch their first keeper. I went about my routine. It was eleven o'clock when we heard the wailing of the police cars running around madly.

Ed Davis, who had a special radio, was the first to know that a heist had taken place at the bank. I didn't see any special alarm from Ed Davis or from George Bone even though both businessmen had put their pouches stuffed with yesterday's business receipts into that bank's outside vault on their way home last night, as was their custom. They weren't a bit worried because this community-owned-and-operated bank belonged to the group known as Federal Deposit Insurance Company which guarantees all the bank's monies.

Smart was the young thief who approached the teller's window with a fake gun and, wearing a short-sleeved red, white, and blue plaid shirt, had no trouble collecting the few thousand dollars the bank had on hand, for the frightened tellers gave up the money readily. The crook politely asked them to lie on the floor while he took his leave with his new riches bulging behind his belt.

Once outside the bank, he calmly walked eastward on First Street while taking off his shirt. He crumbled it up and pressed it down into the middle of a sidewalk plant, of which there were many back then.

He continued to walk the few blocks shirtless until he reached the house at 3 Sixth Avenue S., directly in front of Bone's Jacksonville Beach Fishing Pier, where he pulled out a long-sleeved white shirt and a broad-brimmed straw hat that he had hidden from view in a green plant growing along the sidewalk. The bank robber casually put them on and went back to his fishing on the pier.

It might have worked, except that a roofer was working on top of a property across the street from the place where the bandit removed his shirt. When the repairman saw the man stuff it into a sidewalk plant, he knew he had to reveal this information to the police.

At about twelve thirty, I took walking fees from two young gentlemen coming aboard. Mr. Bone thought they were plainclothesmen. George was ever watchful of the shoes men wore, and when he saw these guys in thick, leather-soled, black shoes he felt certain to call them out. I remember I laughed at him, saying if that were the case, there would be a lot of cops around.

We watched as the two took their time on the pier. They slowly walked all the way to the end, where they seemed to study the entire facility before starting back. When they reached that first booth from the end they stopped to talk to the man fishing there, and that's where we saw one of them throw the handcuffs on the man wearing a white shirt and a big straw hat. Then they marched him off to jail.

33 – Surfers and Their Unending Squabbles

From all I've learned, trouble always brewed between the pier people and the surfing community. By using the word "community" we do not mean that every person who surfed was guilty of harassing the pier's fishermen; there is no such intent. We knew that a greater number of surfers understood the agony the fishermen suffered whenever someone hovered over their line too long. Most fishing people believed that act scared the fish away. Most of the better surfers used appropriate surfing etiquette and proper public behavior. They were a pleasure to watch while in motion. Surfing is a marvelous sport.

However, there were always a number of the "low intellect" class, and especially those whose philosophy was "I don't give a damn about *them*," who made enough trouble for everyone around. They were shameless young brutes who, I think, would beat up their own grandparents without a cause. If we listened to their side of the argument for a minute or two, we would see that most of these offenders were quite ignorant of the whole problem. And as long as ignorance stays in vogue, as long as a surfer thinks he has the right to sit on a fisherman's line, bite his line, or otherwise taunt people on the fishing pier, the problem will continue. It's no more complicated than that.

The war between fishermen and surfers had been going on for some time and seemed to be getting worse. That's because the surfing population had greatly swelled. According to Mr. Williams, he had fewer problems with surfers. That's because there were fewer surfers in 1960 when the pier was new. Williams said he had to call the police on "a couple of occasions because someone was overly intoxicated and unruly," but early surfers paid more attention to local ordinances back then. He said the Jacksonville Beach Police told him to hang a sign, "Keep 400 feet away from the pier," in several places along the bottom edge of the pier, on the north as well as on the south side. "We had little if any trouble after that," according to Mr. Williams, regarding surfing problems of yesteryear.

Since then, surfing has become an industry. Surf shops have sprung up along the entire length of the Atlantic seaboard, especially at Florida's coastal cities. Shops have opened, selling items associated with the sport such as wet suits, long and short boards, goggles, wax, and chewing gum, all helping the local economy.

By the time George Bone acquired the helm of the pier, at least two dozen surfers sat on their boards in plain view on both sides of the pier whenever the surf was up. Jacksonville's college boys and girls came from a dozen area colleges, as well as from Flagler College and St. Johns River Community College in St. Johns County, and formed teams which held competitive meets with visiting troupes from all over the country.

I remember fishing beside George Bone throughout the 1970s and I never heard a bad word uttered by him against the surfers. He and I watched them, waiting with anxious anticipation for the right swell to catch and ride all the way in to the beach. George admired their grace and agility.

One time I heard him exclaim, "God Almighty! Look at that kid stepping back and forth on his bouncing board and then shoot it through that white curl! Did you see that?" He was fascinated with surfers on that day.

But then there were no complaints from the fishermen on that day either. The surfers were well outside the 400 feet and performing beautifully, with not a troublemaker among them. It was one of many perfect days at Bone's Pier.

Then there would come a day of troubles when fishermen would start complaining and we who were on duty that moment were instructed to call the police and let them handle the situation. I always held out as long as possible, but when it got close to becoming unruly, I admit I usually called them for help.

Most of the time, we could safely bet that it was not a college kid causing the commotion, but more likely one of the roughneck rednecks. We could tell who was looking for trouble by the vocabulary being used by the surfer who was talking back to the complaining people on the pier. They would taunt or actually instigate by daring the threatening fishermen to hit them with a leaded line, and when that happened, would always cry foul and sometimes even try to kill the one on the pier.

Occasionally an argument started between a lady fisher-person and a brawling surfer, and that was usually humorous to witness. It was funny because the lady, with fire and hate in her blazing eyes, would threaten to take the surfboard from the surfer's possession and crack him over the head with it. This happened one day when Mrs. Amelia Ormando, full of hot spit and fire, used this favorite threat on Jimmy Poke, who dared her to try it. She was a woman from the pine-tree-growing business who already knew how to use spicy language and get into a fight. She was not the soft-spoken southern lady commonly known in the South.

"Alright, you little shithead bastard, I'm coming down to get you, you little shithead bastard!" She wound up her reel and leaned her rod against the top rail, and started down to the beach with intent to collar this young surfer. This was her plan. We all wondered, *How would she handle this?* She was really insanely psychotic because the surfer had been sitting on top of her line for a long time.

"F— you, lady!" was the last thing she heard as she readied to go down to the beach.

"I'll f— you alright, you little shithead bastard, but you will wish differently when I get through with you, you little shithead bastard!"

Jimmy Poke was one of the daily guys who usually stayed long enough to state his surfing opinions and then would move on hoping his fellow surfers would pick up where he left off and give the outbursting fishermen more tongue-lashing harassment. Although he was one of the regular people to argue with the fishermen, he was never known to be in an actual physical confrontation with anyone. Everybody on the pier now looked to see what would happen when Amelia got down to his level.

Nothing. Nothing happened. As usual, Jimmy disappeared. When he had seen Amelia coming halfway down the exiting boardwalk, he slid his board under the pier and vanished among other surfers on the far north side of the pier. Amelia, with her chin thrust forward and her mouth blue with anger, strutted to the edge of the water on the south side, looked about, and when she saw no surfer inside the 400-foot ordinance, she came back huffing, puffing, and cursing to resume her fishing.

The police of course had been called because the clerk on duty did not want to see any kind of a brawl, man or woman. When the police finally showed up, everything had quieted down. Even Amelia had lost her fighting spirit and had little to say.

...

"Crazy Doug" Breen was not really crazy, but the guys called him crazy because he did strange and stupid things. For instance, he would throw putrid carrion up on the pier, usually following an extended argument between a fisherman and a surfer. He seemed to know where to find these stinking birds and dead roadkill such as raccoons and possums. He would scrape this ripe offal into a paper bag, bring it to the edge of the pier, usually after dark, and heave it up onto the deck where it would make the place smell like hell for us workers until we hosed the stuff off. He was never caught doing this, but he sure bragged about it to his surfing friends and the source found its way back to us.

Breen was out of high school and not steadily employed. He was not interested in college, most probably because he could not afford to even try it. He lived in an old-time trailer with ailing parents who were on disability. The kid mowed lawns in his neighborhood for his spending money, and during cooler weather he'd bike his way to the Thousand Oaks Golf Course on A1A (where the Tournament Players Club / TPC at Sawgrass is now located). Here he made a few real dollars when he worked. However, Breen was one of the top skilled surfers, with many local trophies to his credit. He was always seen coming or going on the beach. Word was out that he was about to leave home to serve in the US Navy, but as yet he was more of a beach bum than anything else.

Tall and chunky, Breen was a two-hundred-pound young man, an easy-to-see surfer. His physique could be picked out of a gang of surfers a quarter of a mile away. Rarely did he personally harass the fishermen. However, one day while I was out fishing for George Bone's family larder, before my time to go on official duty inside, I personally witnessed Breen mooning all the fishermen and women on the south side of the pier. His full white buttocks stood out in profuse contrast against his two-toned, tanned body.

Honest to God! I couldn't get over seeing him standing on his bouncing board with his blue-flowered trunks down around his left ankle. He was a lot closer than 400 feet from the pier. He passed by right beneath us, in front of all our ladies and gentlemen who were definitely shocked by his act, although there was much laughter.

Nobody yelled at him to get away. Most of us laughed our heads off at his show. It was especially hilarious since we couldn't tell what sex he was. Breen looked more like a girl with a hairy pubic area because the cool water had shrunken his manhood parts completely out of sight.

He made only that one, long, 1,000-foot perfect run. Then, in hip-deep water he pulled up his trunks and marched homeward down the beach with his surfboard under his brown arm.

That was Crazy Doug doing his demented thing to vex the people on the pier.

…

One morning when I came to work on the early shift and stepped outside the tackle shop door, my hair stiffened to see two huge holes burned into the pier's cypress-wood planks. There had been a recent confrontation between the police and some bad-boy surfers who were reportedly fined for disobeying police calls. It was thought that those surfers, or their friends, had thrown Molotov cocktails up on the pier in the dark of nighttime, clearly hoping to see Bone's Pier burned to the ground. (The Molotov cocktail, made with bottles filled with highly inflammable fluids, is named after V. M. Molotov, the Soviet leader who successfully burned German tanks with such bombs during World War II). The pier might have gone down in flames that night, except for the good luck of a night walker on the beach, who saw the blaze starting and called 911. Because the incinerating plot had been discovered early on, hundreds of fishermen had a fine, peaceful day of good fishing instead of experiencing a catastrophe.

…

With personal problems, surfer problems, and mortgage problems converging, George Bone's health began to wane noticeably. He drank his booze with a greater appetite. He now out-drank everyone around. He went through a couple of fifths a day all by himself. He thought he had to drink to keep his health.

"I need the stuff to steady my hand," he yelled back at me when I called him on too much drinking while in my company.

There were times when I could not tolerate his drinking, and there were times when I couldn't blame him for soaking up the paralyzing fluid. I began to ask myself, *What would I do if I had his problems? I think I would be spiking my apple juice a bit too.*

However, Mr. Bone met all his pier mortgage payments despite the annoying fact that he had a "big leak" in his cash receivables. It soon became known that he had sold some of his parental property in North Carolina to satisfy at least one payment. Other times he had help from loans given him privately by his brother, Leaston Bone. And, finally, by selling his Neptune Beach house and using part of that sizable equity to conclude his final pier debt to Mr. Williams, the mortgagee.

In the early 1960s, the Bones had purchased at a small cost a sizable property on Neptune Beach that had quite a bit of wind and weather damage. George and his friend John Ballinger mended, painted, and jazzed up the property to a newness that made it one of the most attractive properties on the local scene, and it grew in equity in a big way as the decades passed.

George hadn't wanted to sell his Neptune Beach house because he had loved living there. It was his idea of a perfect lifestyle—that is, until he was clobbered one midnight and almost killed from a blow to his head.

As with most properties in Neptune Beach, the side entrance to this beach house stood very close to its neighboring building, about twenty feet apart. It was believed that the aggressor was hiding in the shadows of the neighbor's alcove waiting for George to stagger home. He walloped George on the head with a blunt object, which was found to be a huge iron clamshell. The clamshell was found on the driveway near George's doorway. George told us he was able to open his front door and yell into his house for his wife to call the law.

"Then I passed out," George said. He only remembered hearing footsteps running down towards the beach, but never saw any part of the assailant or assailants to enable identification. He told the police he had no concrete idea as to who it was that had lain in wait to attack.

"Who in hell is after me with the intent to kill?" he asked of us at the pier. This episode badly scared George Bone, and it made it easier for him to sell his beloved beach home. Within twenty-four hours of the attack he had made up his mind it would be best to relocate from the busy, spooky beach. Because his house was in cream-puff condition it was easy to sell for top dollar. At the time, local beach properties were much in demand, especially handsome places. The property was sold and closed within a month.

The identity of the hoodlum was never learned. George thought if it was not a surfer, then it had to be the son or sons of a man whom he had recently fired. He had let this employee go because Mr. Poole encouraged him to believe this clerk was definitely the clever thief who was stealing cash from the business. As a matter of fact, George felt good after he had fired Carmelo Ausli; there was immediately a larger tally after his dismissal. But then came these vicious attacks on his life following that particular firing. Dick Poole claimed also that he thought the Auslis were behind these terrible assaults.

"That's the way those dagos operate," Poole said, to soothe his good friend, as if Poole was an expert on such things.

"Yeah," agreed George Bone, shaking his head as he thought back to the *Godfather* movies, "I think you're right. They are a vicious race of people, alright."

In hindsight, it is distressing how much influence Dick Poole had over George. Although I later demonstrated to Ann Bone that Poole was taking cash from the pier till, it was unknown at that time and thus the Bones had to sell their property on Neptune Beach. When I think about the "leak" from the cash drawer bringing about the health issues incurred by George as a result of his imbibing, the subsequent marital problems for him and his wife, and the firing of Carmelo Ausli all due to the actions (unknown at the time) of Mr. Poole, I am greatly saddened.

Until my discussion with Mrs. Bone, I thought that Mr. Poole was a partner of Mr. Bone's in this pier business, so often was his taking of monies.

George let everyone know, whether they wished him good or evil, that he would pay any price, bear any burden, meet any hardship, to protect his friendship with his buddy, Dick Poole. That's how much he was involved with his friend. He had a blind belief in his goodness.

As I became aware of Poole's taking cash, I also noticed he had increased his visits to the pier. As George became less and less able, Mr. Poole became more and more aggressive in his presence. I witnessed many times George complaining to Mr. Poole that the crowd did not match the money in the till, and Mr. Poole would lift George's spirits, saying things like: "George, they will come. There's still time, they will come. Don't worry, George, don't worry." And on his friend's advice, George would stop worrying.

....

SURFERS HOLD FORUM

From a recent public forum we were able to glean some firsthand, first-person attitudes about the ongoing battle between the surfers and their adversaries, the fishermen.

This surfer's voice is heard over and over again: *The fishermen want the space along the pier to catch fish, while the growing number of surfers want to catch better waves.*

This fisherman tells it like he sees it: *Fishermen are at odds with surfers over the space around the pier. Some surfers say the pier is the reason for the best waves—but fishermen on the pier say the wave riders are crossing the line when they are closer than 400 feet.*

A new idea hits the post from a young surfer: *Just had a thought. The surfers might be able to get the city to build us a new pier that is not as long as this one and where fishing is prohibited on it or around it, from shore or from a boat. I don't know if it would create the favorable environment that the Jax Beach Pier does for surfing, but it's worth a shot. Like I said, it's just a thought.*

A voice from a fishing lady: *Sometimes, a dozen surfers were riding our lines and fishhooks. There is a Jacksonville Beach ordinance that requires all to stay 400 feet from the pier, but it's rarely enforced. This is what really causes fishermen to get huffy.*

Another surfer wants everyone to know: *The fishermen on the pier want their space beside the pier to catch fish, while the surfers merely want to catch waves there.*

Here is the voice of a philosopher with a brainstorm (mistakes are his): *We have been dealing with this in Fern for years all you gotta is walk on the pier knock one of them out and they'll shut up!!!!*

Here is another message from one who knows much and has super-thoughts (mistakes are his): *What would fishermen do if there was no pier? They can be creative. The pier does not attract fish as it does create good waves. There have been surfers longer than there have been piers. Surfers should not have to move in order to give fishermen there spot. I'm pretty sure that Florida has a whole lotta coastline.*

This is a note from a fisherman who also surfs: *Actually, the pier does attract fish. They like to hang around structures of any type. I'm pretty sure piers have been around for a long damn time, longer than surfing has been popular anyway. Not trying to defend the jackasses that hurl weights at people or anything, but the pier was built as a "fishing pier." I surf and I fish and I think the fighting over the two is petty. All we surfers have to do is keep 400 feet away from the sides of the pier and the argument would end.*

Another fisherman sounds off: *There is a very good reason to fish around close to the shore and to the pier. That's where the fish are feeding. The cuts, sloughs, and holes are the reason for our casting about. I agree that deliberate targeting of anyone is unlawful and a despicable act that should be dealt with and abolished. However, most pier fishermen that I know do not engage in this kind of sport. Problem is not all fishermen know how to cast well. Even when all the unlawful acts are dealt with, there still will be a lot of wayward casting that will happen. If a foolish surfer is close enough and is beneath a wayward cast he may lose an eye. We have been arguing over this issue for decades and things haven't changed. Perhaps a different approach is in order. How about an attitude change for openers?*

This observing citizen asks for more understanding on both sides: *There are also laws to protect citizens against battery. Someone getting in the way of a person fishing may be unlawful, but it is no excuse for people to take the law into their own hands and start doling out corporal punishment. I have seen surfers have hooks, weights, and lines thrown at them. And I have seen those who throw laugh at the idea of injuring others. I believe there is too much animosity on both sides and not enough understanding with either side.*

Ban fishermen from the pier, is the call from this surfer: *We know who these few fishermen are who intentionally target surfers with hooks and lead sinkers. It seems like you are protecting them with a "prove it" attitude when you know who they are and what their true intent is. Why are we playing word games? Bar them from the pier and end this issue and let's surf.*

This sounds like a father figure who is angry with the city officials as well as the surfers: *I will simply state that when one of you gets knocked in the head and killed by a lead sinker because you did not adhere to the warnings that are posted on both sides of the pier, or did not have enough common sense to understand the dangers of surfing in the immediate area where several dozen amateur fishermen are casting their lines about; and then a lawsuit for millions of dollars shows up from the parents to sue the city of Jacksonville Beach because the mayor, the city manager, police, and lifeguards don't have the kahunas to stand up and try to resolve this issue, and the citizens and taxpayers want to know why, then you can tell them that little Billy wanted to be one with Mother Nature and surf next to the pier because the waves were six inches higher.*

A young surfer tells it like he thinks it is: *We surfers contribute quite a bit to the community. Ever seen a fisherman for an autism event? How about fishermen sponsoring a beach cleanup event? How about fishermen sponsoring a youth camp for disadvantaged youths? Me neither. But surfers sponsor these events all the time. We also pay for parking, we support local restaurants and bars after a surf session, buy gear from local surf shops, hold contests, and support local cultural events at establishments and museums.*

Surfing is now big business, as reported here by the SIMA: *Nearly 40 percent of all East Coast surfing occurs in Florida waters, and* *despite tough economic times the surfing industry remains resilient, showing $7.22 billion in sales in 2008 and considerable growth over the past years. This report is furnished according to research done by the Surf Industry Manufacturing Association.*

Believing the ocean pumps better closer to the pier, some surfers still worry the fishermen as they ride their boards over lines, preventing people from catching their seafood dinner.

34 – Venomous Attack on George

Mr. and Mrs. George Bone bought another distressed property on the Intracoastal Waterway in Palm Valley, where they moved to escape their beach and surfer problems. But danger still followed George. A live, four-foot rattlesnake found its way into his station wagon. That good morning, George asked me to take his wheels and run to downtown Jacksonville to pick up the current dog track racing forms, an errand I often performed. On this particular morning, however, I was involved with a project and didn't leave as quickly as George expected, and so he decided to go instead.

George never locked his car. Somebody with malice in his heart for George knew this and waited to plant that freshly caught poisonous viper in George's vehicle that very morning. A bite from a robust diamondback such as this could have been fatal, but it was not to be.

George told us: "It was near the Tower Building on A1A when I was slowing down for the red light there, and I happened to look to my right and my eyes felt a quiver of movement. I looked down, and there, to my hell-of-a-surprise, on the front passenger seat sat a goddamn pink-colored rattler with its tail raised and buzzing away. It must have just shed its skin recently and was fresh and ready to strike me. I braked my car and the sudden stop threw the snake on the front floor. I opened my door and threw myself out of my car onto the street. I think that with the quick kicking I did to get out of the goddamn car, I must have picked up the rattler with my boot and threw it out of the car at the same time. So there I sat on my goddamn ass watching this goddamn pink rattler swishing away as it hurried across A1A towards the greenery, not far to the west side of the road—and a car coming from north to south ran over it and squashed it flat as a board as I sat there and watched."

Apparently disappointed because their last trick didn't work, the spooky phantom tried it again. A week later, George opened his mailbox and a small, dark-colored diamondback shot its head out and fell to the ground, and disappeared among the blooming blue morning glories. Again, George lucked out from a possible lethal injury, but this last attempt to hurt him was enough to put George in the hospital with chest pains. He was kept for several days.

Distraught, Ann Bone called their daughter in Atlanta and suggested Rhonda should consider coming back home to take over the management of their fishing pier business.

Newly divorced, Rhonda was in need of a change in atmosphere, so she accepted the challenge—providing her parents agreed to let her have full say on the pier's ways and means. Rhonda, the one and only child of the Bones, was smart enough to know there could only be one boss—one sober boss on this job—otherwise it could turn out to be a greater confusion and chaos, and she didn't want any part of that kind of life. They gave Rhonda full rein. They knew she was an adroit individual, especially since she had all that business knowledge from ten years in her office position in Atlanta.

George wasn't happy about giving up the captainship of the pier, especially since he had enjoyed being the boss and leader of this fascinating facility more than any other thing that he had ever done. However, he knew he wasn't up to handling the business. He felt he would get well and strong enough in a few weeks and would rule equally beside his daughter.

Ann was thrilled with the prospects of having her beautiful and loving daughter and her two adorable grandchildren at hand again. Rhonda said it would be a couple of months before she would be able to relocate back to Jacksonville Beach, but she was coming; thank God, she was coming back home where she was badly needed.

35 – The Davises Are Giving Up

    The restaurant was up for rental again. Ed Davis and his wife were separating after five years of hard work at the pier. Davis said it was his wife who decided she wanted out of the marriage because she intended going back to an old Chicago flame whose profession was raising Great Dane dogs. Davis was ready to quit the chophouse enterprise at the pier due to the late hours and hard work it took to keep the place profitable. Mrs. Davis disappeared quietly, while Ed Davis, with his hired help, continued with the same course of action, making coffee and keeping the fishermen happy with his chili, fish sandwiches, and stuffed pork chop dinners until the Bones found a new entrepreneur. Ed Davis did not seem unhappy about the big change in his life, though it made me sad to see there had been a serious discord with these people whom I liked very much.

    It was a matter of several weeks before Ann Bone found a couple of businessmen who were ready, willing, and able to take over the facility. By chance, she mentioned the restaurant's availability to Jesse Grant, one of her craft suppliers in St. Augustine, and Jesse happened to know of a guy who was searching for a location to open a snack-shack business. Ann asked Jesse to contact this fellow and advise him to call her for more particulars. He did and that's how things worked out so quickly.

    So the new people showed up to inspect what was available before they agreed to sign on the dotted line. This time it was a pair of college-educated men who had formed a partnership to run a business. Jake Brown, a tall, pleasant-looking man, was dressed in a fresh, gray, Air Force jumpsuit and a gray baseball cap. The main character of the pair, he was a retired US Air Force major, a flyer with a straight back who walked rapidly about, looking into every crack and crevice of the place. "Jake," as he was called by his business associate, didn't miss anything. His gray-blue eyes saw everything at once that day. His partner stood in the center of the place and turned himself only as much as needed to follow Brown's commentary.

A retired food broker, Frank Smelansky, a tall, robust man with a pronounced red nose and a large head with a shock of curly brown hair, looked on as his partner spoke. It was plain to see this associate was not prepared to do any kind of manual work. He wore a sports jacket and well-pressed gray slacks, a long-sleeved white shirt with a vivid blue silk necktie, as if he was expecting to go to a cocktail party. Perhaps he had already been to one, because Smelansky looked on with a dreamy countenance reminiscent of W. C. Fields as he tripped around that day. We referred to these newcomers as "Arty" and "Farty."

They agreed to rent the place and moved in quickly. Several workers spent a whole day repainting the entire restaurant from top to bottom with a bilious light-green color they called "sea foam green." They threw out every piece of the warm décor brought in by the Davises, including the dust-catching, timeworn Stars and Stripes that had hung high on the back wall above the plate-glass windows, which was the hallway wall of the restaurant. In its place, a tiny American flag was set on the counter near their register, where everyone who came in could see it.

The kitchen was power washed and steam cleaned from top to bottom and the walls were painted white. The twenty wooden oak tables out front were recovered with a sheet of green-and-white checkered oilcloth which was smoothly tacked down underneath with a staple gun. The twelve counter stools were unscrewed, removed, and stored in a huge closet in the back of the poolroom. It was obvious the new guys didn't care to have people hovering over their coffee cups for hours on end, and they removed the stools which definitely invited this comfort.

Except for the area where the cash register was installed and the counter where people would place their corndog and hamburger orders, the bigger part of the counter across the front of the kitchen was raised a bit higher and recovered with a light-colored paneling. This part of the counter was loaded high with impulse-buying items: candy bars, bags of popcorn, Slim Jims, and chewing items such as gum and tobacco products.

The restaurant took on a sterile atmosphere overnight. Nothing indicated that these new people would cook chili, make fish chowder, or serve stuffed pork chop dinners. They did, however, specialize in a good breakfast program served with sanitary paper napkins and plastic tableware and paper coffee cups. In comparison to what the Davises had going, neither one of these new people cared to work any more than was absolutely necessary.

Jake, the head boss, was a health nut; it was plain to see that right off. Like Ed Davis he was remarried to a beautiful younger woman and needed to watch himself. He let us know he was weight conscious. The first day we met, he was recovering from dental surgery. He said it was done to permanently prevent bad breath from gum disease like gingivitis, which he claimed he didn't yet have. He said he took several vitamins each day and exercised every day of his life. He drank a little wine, he said, but didn't touch the more potent liquors. We wondered how he was going to get along with George, who lately was generally in a stupored, mine-boggled condition.

Jake kept the restaurant and the restrooms spotless and expected his partner to do the same. Jake worked from eight o'clock in the morning until three o'clock, then Smelansky expertly took over the cooking of hamburgers and corndogs. In the height of the summer season they closed promptly at nine o'clock each evening, saying they were not interested in having problems with nighttime beer drinkers.

They made a go of it, especially in the summer months, but during the cooler periods they hardly made enough to pay for their light bill. None of us could see where they made a decent profit. They never seemed to be happy. These two college-educated entrepreneurs rarely had a smile on either face. We thought maybe they expected a full house every day, but they hardly ever attracted even a good crowd.

36 – The Mascot's Day

George was getting better and was now expressing the desire to have a pig for the pier's mascot. He didn't take this up with his wife or with his managing daughter, but expressed this desire to Bud Jackson, the new young man who worked on the pier by day. Jackson liked George so much that he went down near Palm Valley to a hog farm and stole a sleeping white young shoat away from its groggy mother. He taped the squealing piglet's mouth shut with masking tape and carried it away one dark midnight.

It may have been one of George Bone's childhood memories that got picked up by his present-day psyche and demanded the fulfillment of this desire, but no one will ever know for sure what went on in his head at that time. All I knew for certain was that George was exceedingly happy with the gift of the piggy. He thanked Jackson over and over again for bringing him this sweet little mascot. He did ask where it came from, and when Jackson said, "The pet shop," it satisfied George enough not to question further.

"Now help me train this little sucker, will you?"

"Sure, George, certainly," agreed Jackson.

The mascot lasted for barely a day, but it was an exciting day, to say the least. When Ann and Rhonda showed up at ten o'clock, they of course showed displeasure in finding the screaming piglet on the pier. George took the little stranger for a walk into Ann's gift shop and it immediately scooched into a squat and exploded a juicy bowel movement on Ann's freshly vacuumed carpet.

Ann began to weep, and George began to scrape up what he could onto some newspaper.

"No, George!" Ann screamed. "We now have to have some soapy boiling water to shampoo this rug to get the smell out of here."

"Okay, okay, Ann. I'll do that, don't you worry." George was panting for breath, the pig was squealing to high heavens, and Ann closed her shop until it was scrubbed.

George went to boil a bucket of water in the tackle shop, and Jackson reappeared with an empty fifty-gallon drum. They placed this metallic thing, open on top, on its side, out against the side of the pier-building. This metal drum was intended for the mascot's home.

When they put the pig into the cylinder, it went berserk and screamed even louder than before. Jackson removed the animal from the tank and held it in his arms like a baby, which quieted it some. Then he decided to give this howler a bath. When he turned up the hose and began the bath, that piggy nearly turned itself inside out with fright. It cried unmercifully.

"I think it's hungry," George said.

"What shall we feed it?" Jackson asked.

"Go over to the feed store and ask them for advice," George pleaded.

Within the hour Jackson was back with a fifty-pound bag of something called "middlings," a powdery substance that is like pabulum for baby pigs. Jackson mixed a pint of this stuff into a gallon of warm water and we watched this baby pig slurp it down. Its belly grew wide and fat and it soon lay down in the shade of the big drum and went to sleep.

In the meantime, because it was a nice day, the pier was filling up with fishermen. I noticed that the two redneck brothers were coming aboard today. We recognized them because they both always wore a newish-looking pair of old-fashioned blue denim overalls, the kind that had wide straps hooked on at shoulder level. They fished regularly every other week. They were a quiet pair who took everything home that they caught, including the trash fish such as catfish and bony ladyfish.

George spent a good hour washing Ann's carpet. After he spent time scrubbing it twice with suds, the shop still smelled strange, kind of like a barn smells in the summertime. They hoped the smell would air out and disappear in a short time.

Anyhow, George had quieted Ann down. She was no longer mad at him. He sat in the captain's chair beside her stool and discussed how wonderful it was to finally have a real mascot on this pier.

"It will be good for our business," George told Ann.

She told him not to bring that noisy little critter into her shop again, and he agreed.

After lunch George decided to take the mascot for a walk out to the end of the pier. That is what his intensions were. That little pig knew it was walking on something up in the air, but it could not figure out the noise below, and refused to follow George's footsteps. It began to cry bloody murder and George chose to turn around. On his way back to the tackle shop, the thought occurred to George to take his piggy into the restaurant to show it off to those in there, and maybe buy an ice cream cone for the pet. The pig was now following and noisily grunting beside George Bone.

As he opened the door to enter, I saw from the tackle shop counter that Jake Brown was rushing forward and yelling at the top of his voice, "Don't you dare bring that stinking critter into this restaurant!"

George either didn't hear the man, or thought he was kidding and proceeded to go in. Jake rushed forward and grabbed George by the shoulder, spun him around, and pushed him back out of the restaurant, into the hall. Jake held the door open long enough for the mascot to trot back out after George's heels, and Jake slammed the door shut with a bang.

George turned around quickly and wanted to confront Jake in some sort of dialogue.

Jake opened the door a tiny bit and shook his fist at George, and said, "I meant what I said, and if you want me to call the cops, just you try to come in here again with that pig. If I were you, I'd get rid of that dirty animal right now."

The door slammed again.

At that precise moment the two redneck brothers were already inside the pier-house, on their way home, and they saw and heard what was going on. The first brother stepped up to George fast and asked George if he wanted to get rid of that pig, and if so, he and his brother would be glad to take it away. George nodded yes and motioned them to take it.

The redneck brothers may not have had a decent fish in their bucket, but they fell into at least a week's worth of pork roasts that day.

Jackson was down in the parking lot repairing a pothole when he heard something that sounded like a piglet screeching. He looked over and saw a man quickly stop the squealing with a blunt blow of a tire iron, and before Jackson could catch up with them, the twins were on their way out and gone!

37 – A Surfer Strikes

The surfers were always creating problems. It was only a matter of time before something dreadful was to come along. It had been building for a long time, and the day finally arrived when the old fisherman, Scot Marvin, hit surfer Tony Santino's well-waxed surfboard with a heavy lead sinker. This aroused Tony's South Philadelphian Sicilian ire, which put this surfer in serious trouble.

"What the f— do you think you're doing?" screamed Santino, with murder resounding in his voice.

"You are sitting over my line here, and you're 400 yards too close to this pier, so move the hell out farther or I'll pop another one off your head," said Scot, who was fixing to throw another piece of lead out onto the surfer.

Scot was equally steamed. This handsome, well-built, senior black man was hearty enough not to fear anyone. One of the regulars on the pier, he was a serious fisherman. He was also prepared with lots of weights to hurl out at anyone who came into his range. He actually tried to really hurt one of the offending surfers.

However, it soon became clear that the surfer's intent was not to retreat and go farther out. He started leaving the water while loudly muttering terrible obscenities. Witnesses saw Santino leave the water and run to his car parked in the pier's parking lot, open his trunk, and pull out his tire iron. They saw him wrap the iron in a towel, and jump up onto the pier's ramp on the run. In the meantime several of the daily fishermen on the pier saw Santino coming and they moved closer to where Scot was located.

Another witness was on his way into the tackle shop and reported what he saw to a pier employee, Ronnie Juniper. Juniper called the police and then headed out to see what he could do to prevent an encounter.

On his way out to the pier, not far behind Santino, Juniper saw the mad surfer's rushing approach to the fisherman's station. Yelling and cussing, Santino first picked up Marvin's expensive rod and reel and tossed the prized combo overboard into the ocean, to everyone's surprise. The surfer's arm with the iron tool was already raised to clobber Scot. Juniper rushed up between the two, trying to calm the surfer, when Santino swung his tool and artfully struck Juniper on the forehead. The peacemaker's head wound opened, spurting blood, and the pier's deck quickly began to look like a battle zone.

Now seeing blood gushing from Juniper's hairline down over his eyes and face, the pier's observing fishermen promptly jumped on Santino and threw him down on the deck planks. A couple of them sat on top of the struggling young man to hold him for the police, who were already on the way up.

Witnesses said that Santino's cries could be heard into the next county. He used the vilest vocabulary as he protested against the fishermen who were holding him down. He almost struggled free when Juniper, not realizing his own situation, decided to help hold him, and he too sat down on the struggling surfer.

"Hey dude, get the f— off of me," Santino protested. "Your f— blood is running down on me," he shrieked and squealed pathetically.

In spite of his piercing screams, he was thusly held as the police arrived on the scene. Then, humorous to the fishermen and everyone standing by, Santino began to loudly complain to the police how he was "mistreated" and his body was "nearly ripped apart."

"Where were you fishing?" asked the deputy sheriff. "Show me where you were fishing."

"I wasn't fishing, dude," gasped the subdued one.

"Then what are you doing on this fishing pier?"

"Dude, I was surfing, when—"

The policeman slapped handcuffs on the screaming man.

Ronnie Juniper was rushed to the hospital, where they stopped his bleeding and put several dozen stitches in the peace-seeker's scalp. Santino was also examined at the hospital and then released to the police, who took the twenty-eight-year-old surfer to jail and charged him with simple battery and petit theft, both misdemeanors. The theft charge resulted from the fisherman's rod and reel that Santino had thrown into the sea.

The fishermen could readily see how lucky it turned out for Santino. If his tire iron had caught Ron Juniper on the side temple or on top of the soft spot in his skull with the same impact, the charge could have been murder, or at least "assault with intent to kill," and not a misdemeanor charge.

As it was, the State Attorney's Office said hypothetically if the tire iron was yet found and produced as evidence, the charge could change to a felony. Santino could be recharged with aggravated battery with a deadly weapon, with considerable more punishment.

Some witnesses alleged the surfer was seen wrapping his tire iron in a towel and then they saw him carry it up on the pier with him. Fishermen on the scene said they saw Santino throw the instrument overboard after he struck Juniper. The fact that the pier employee wound up with the vicious wound indicated a hard instrument was used to cause this bloody damage, but the weapon was never located.

One does not have to be a scientist to see this suggests that someone from the perpetrator's family, or an empathetic surfer, walked about in the low tide's shallow waters until the tire iron was found and made certain it would not become the important clue to this crime. Santino lucked out, as Ron did not press charges, and there was no jail time penalty to this case.

38 – The Runaway Barge Problem

With all the troubles George had, it was enough to make him sick, but the surfers were small potatoes compared to several maverick seagoing crafts that went on the loose.

In December of 1980 a chemical-carrying barge broke from its lines at sea and ran aground a mile north of the pier. Then the tugboat that was trying to free the barge became a victim of the sandbar, but it was rocked free and taken out of the way. The barge, now free and loose, began to drift southward towards the fishing pier.

"Holus bolus! If that ocean freight hauler bumps into this pier," Ann said to George, "we've had it."

They watched the bulky shape drift slowly towards them in the strong surf-side current. To them, it looked like it was suddenly going to be the end of their fishing pier business.

Fortunately, the agent for the barge quickly dispatched a Jacksonville marine salvage company to the scene just in time, and the pier was not threatened. But it caused an endless tourist attraction, especially for the photo-maniacs.

…

Three years later, on November 21, 1984, it happened again when a huge 235-foot barge loaded to capacity with 121 colossal containers of fresh foodstuffs broke loose from its towboat out in the deep ocean, and with a forceful current began drifting southward towards the beach and Bone's Pier. This carrier was also owned by Gulf Fleet Marine out of New Orleans. Again the crowds came from far and near to watch the phenomenon and to take pictures.

Now, George and his wife stood beside their daughter, Rhonda, watching the peril about to happen and they were beside themselves with anxiety.

"If that son of a bitch drifts into this pier, it's as good as gone," whimpered George Bone.

He was right, for if the heavily loaded barge merely so much as touched the twenty-five-year-old wooden pier it would have been crushed and moved southward with the barge, as sticks and splinters.

The Jacksonville Beach Police knew heavy equipment was on its way, and cordoned off an area to hold back the tourists, who started to pile into town. Police roped off a few square blocks, providing enough space for easier access in which emergency crews could operate.

George and his family felt a little bit easier when the Coast Guard finally appeared with their heavy anchors, which skilled young divers would use to tie the unruly barge to the ocean floor to stop its roll. At this time, it had been estimated that the barge would collide with the pier within three to four hours, judging from the speed it was grooving southward.

This was the amount of information I was able to report here, but only recently (2012) we learned the truth, which was different from what the media reported at the time.

Rhea Smith, my daughter's longtime friend, told us it was her father, Latham Smith, who was responsible for saving Bone's Jax Beach Pier, as well as that huge, troublesome oceangoing barge that was on the loose.

According to Rhea, just after dark the Smith family were about to have a chunk of pecan-pumpkin pie for dessert when the US Coast Guard phoned their dad asking for his assistance to stop a runaway barge that was threatening to smack into Bone's Jax Beach Pier. Pleasantly, he accepted the invitation—and after these many years he still has a scar on his hand from this long-ago ordeal, Rhea said.

Sea Captain Latham Smith of Smith Maritime, Green Cove Springs, Florida, is a Master Mariner and the most respected and experienced of salvage and maritime minds in the Western Hemisphere. He borrowed a wet suit from a neighbor, threw a stretch of thin rope and a length of hawser into his pickup, and headed for Jacksonville Beach, about fifty miles due east.

Latham was on the scene within the hour. He stood on the edge of the ocean and looked out at the frightful sight, and wondered why in the world those professional divers were coming in. He soon discovered that they were unable to get aboard the barge, were completely exhausted, and had to give up.

Rhea said her father was a veteran of countless rescues, and was a powerful swimmer and diver in his own right. If anyone could find a way, he would. He had been called upon to manage the hawsers and gear and to technically secure this runaway barge to the bottom of the Atlantic Ocean. He stood appraising the situation by staring at the sea. According to Rhea, her father had to make an attempt. He gave a signal that he was going to try to board that barge, and away he went over one wave and then another and another ....

The crowd of onlookers, she said, could not get over seeing her skinny, tough, forty-four-year-old dad scramble onto that wildly bucking flat boat, pulling off what the Jacksonville pros were not able to do.

"But that's my dad!" Rhea lovingly bragged. "There were electrical cables on that barge that were powering several large frozen containers called reefers, which had lost power. Dad insisted on fixing this situation and in the dark and wet condition aboard that vessel he was nearly electrocuted. He managed to restore the power, but his hand was painfully burned. They took him to the hospital for treatment. The goggles he was wearing were pitted from electric sparks ...."

And so, here in the year of 2012 we went to Green Cove Springs to ask Captain Latham Smith what he remembered about that day back in 1984. We discovered that he has a perfectly vivid memory.

These are Capt. Latham Smith's words concerning his day at the site of the pier's rescue. Here we learn even more, according to this original source:

> When I arrived at the scene, there was a lot going on already. Navy and Coast Guard personnel were all over the place. The northeast wind was howling in the 50-mph range; it was cold, wet, and rainy. The full wrath of a Force 7 gale was hammering the coast, pounding the shore mercilessly. We had to shout to be heard. The ocean was in full fury.

That ornery barge could be seen 300 feet offshore, unrestrainedly slamming around, banging and crashing down onto the sandbar. This bar was keeping it from climbing onto the beach. I could see it was first high in the air, then it was crashing down onto the sandbar by the ten- and twelve-foot waves. The water was boiling and swirling and causing back eddies to suck the barge backward, then huge breakers again lifted the bulky structure high up and slammed it down again onto the sandbar.

The shudder of the barge slams into the earth below could be felt by everyone standing on the beach. The shrieking wind and the monstrous surf created a noise that was deafening. It was a powerful scene to witness and we wondered what the people of the pier were thinking at that point in time.

It was clear that the only chance to rescue the pier was to somehow get a line onto the barge and secure it to the beach until the weather calmed and it could be towed away.

Big searchlights were brought in and focused on the barge. The Coast Guard and Navy dive team, the best divers in Northeast Florida, were brought in. These young, strong 23- to 26-year-olds, experts in the sea, lost no time as they jumped into their wet suits and started their task of getting a line onto the barge. A crane was set into position to anchor the barge to the beach.

I watched as the assault on the wild surf began. For three long hours, the powerful young divers fought relentlessly to get a line on the barge, but they could not do it. Time after time they tried, man after man they struggled against the overpowering surf, whipped by winds and waves, thrown back over and over and over again until finally, exhausted, spent, completely overcome, they were forced to give up in defeat and retreated to the beach in despair. The barge continued bucking and moving southward towards the pier.

I was sorry these men were defeated. They certainly tried their utmost. However, I stood there thinking that there is usually a pattern in every situation and if you watch it long enough, you could see it, and if you can see it, you can use it to good advantage. It was now about two o'clock in the morning.

I found the waves were coming in sets of seven, then there was a pause, followed again by seven big whitecaps. I gave a signal that I was going to try reaching the barge. I tied a thin rope to my waist and I stood waiting and counting. At the precise moment I raced into the surf and fought my way out to the barge. I got to a place where I could touch bottom on the sandbar. Then I positioned myself between the barge and the surf. I found that although the barge was thrashing about wildly out of control, the sandbar was keeping it from moving too fast towards the beach, which was to my advantage.

The one thing I remember most about that night so long ago was the resounding noise out there. The *sound* of it all was deafening, and surprising to me. The howling of the wind and the crashing surf, plus the pounding of the barge, plus the heavy chain slamming against the hollow steel sounded like total fury. It was so loud I could hardly hear myself think. That and the fact that when the barge came pounding down onto the sandbar, I could actually feel the water tremble from the force of it all. There was some big-time power in that barge action. It was intense!

The barge was scouring out a huge gouge in the sandbar, digging its way southward. But once I got close to the barge, the gouge and the eddies created a deep trough that was way too deep to stand in. The side of the barge was twelve feet high. And there was a chain that had come loose on board which was hanging off the side that, if I could get hold of it, I could use to scramble up onto the deck. But the problem was the chain was being thrown against the side of the barge with such frenzy that if I misjudged it, it could smash my skull.

Nevertheless, since I was already this far I knew that the chain was my only chance to get myself onto that barge. I could see that trying to lasso one of the bollards was simply impossible and using the chain was my only way to go.

It was eight to ten feet from the edge of the sandbar to the side of the barge. It was dangerous as hell just being there, with all the churning surf and unpredictability of the wave action and the backwash of the eddies and all. I was able to get within approximately eight feet of the barge. I was getting tired and I realized that I would have to go soon if I was going to do it. So I counted off a fresh set of seven waves, dug my feet down in the sand as hard as I could, and crouched down. The barge came slamming down and pounded the sandbar with a shudder. The chain slammed forcefully against the sidewall. At that exact instant I leapt out as hard as I could. Luckily I hit the side of the barge and glommed onto it just like a tree frog. I grabbed for that chain, caught it, and held onto it. The rest was fairly easy. I simply scrambled up that chain like a monkey goes up a tree. It all happened in a flash of a moment while the adrenaline was pumping big-time. For me, it was an incredible moment to be able to help secure the barge to the beach.

The other thing I remember so well was seeing the lawyers gathering at the hotel. I can see it all again, even now. There were four of 'em who piled in, one after the other, eating donuts and pointing their fingers while telling us all about the runaway barge.

I remember thinking that there's going to be a lot of yapping about who did this and who did that before all this ends.

And it was a long time before they sorted things out, and a long time before I got paid for my work that day.

39 – The End of Poole

One bright Saturday the pier was loaded with people. I had opened that morning, along with George. About eight o'clock Mr. Poole came up to me, but I told him not to interfere with my time. He didn't try to assume authority. He hung around straightening the rental rack and rearranging the tackle wall, knowing it pleased George to no end. This was how he usually waited for the hour when I'd sign out and he'd take over the cash register work. That was what he did for George in the past; he simply automatically helped out, and George was always appreciative as all get-out.

That day George had company. One of George's cousins, a retired US Army captain, and his wife dropped by as they were visiting from North Carolina. And although I rarely saw her inside the tackle shop, because of their company Ann Bone came inside the counter and they were all sitting on stools in the space between the tackle hangers and the sink, beside George's open bar. The ladies were drinking plain ginger ale, but, as usual, the men were into straight whiskey. George had caught a nice, big, fat speckled sea trout earlier that morning and had it cleaned and filleted. He asked if I would mind frying it up for his company. He liked the way I coated fish with Old Bay–seasoned flour, egg, and cracker meal, and he knew it would be a big hit with his cousins.

So I began to heat up the spider to fry the fish. Mr. Poole took right over, telling George, "I've got some time to help out here, so you can enjoy your company." Appreciatively, George turned around to continue chatting with his cousins. Those people really liked to talk about "back home stuff."

Two conversations were going on; the women were into ladies' talk, while the men were into North Carolina's people and more boisterous interests. Ann was sitting beside me, facing front, and as it so happened, because he was in her full view she saw Mr. Poole receiving customers. She observed him put something in his right pants pocket at the same moment he was stamping a customer's wrist with his left hand. She thought that was a strange chain of action, but said nothing at that particular moment.

I turned the fillets and saw they were getting brown and crusted and began to draw them from the pan onto a plate with a couple of paper towels to absorb any excess oil.

The men were enjoying their whiskey and funny stories and were laughing up one comical memory after another. Occasionally Mr. Poole would turn halfway around and yell out a line or two to the discussion, like this: "Have you heard about the two guys who met at the bar and one said to the other, 'What the heck is the phase of the moon, is it waning or waxing or what,' and the other one said, 'I don't know, I'm not from this neighborhood.' " Poole was a master at throwing witty quips.

I had a moment before the next batch was ready and I turned to see who the customers were that were being admitted. As I looked on, I saw Mr. Poole bend down to where we kept a paper bag with rolls of quarter, dimes, and pennies. I plainly saw him put a roll of dimes into the cash register's drawer—and slip another roll of dimes into his right pants pocket as he carried on a lively conversation with the customer.

I looked over at Ann, who seemed to be in shock, and I asked, "Did you see that?"

She nodded and yelled out, "Yes, I did!"

I was so glad to hear that, because until that moment my words to her had been an unproven fairy tale. I went about my business with the fish. I put the plate of fillets on the sink's counter along with a jar of fresh tartar sauce, and turned to clean up the spider and sink area.

I noticed that Ann had pulled George into the enclosed back room behind the shop, behind us. It was a tiny resting area with only room for a single cot and a small set of drawers. I knew Ann was having a private conversation with George, and I also knew what she was discussing. She was telling him what she and I had seen.

They were gone only a minute or two when they reappeared. Ann apologized to the cousins and began another conversation. The cousins thanked me for the delicious repast, but George seemed distracted. He was a man who loved fried fish, and especially the way I seasoned and cooked it, but he didn't even look at it.

Instead he slowly went to the showcase and took out a new Bowie knife, and soon enough we were all privy to what he was up to. At first I thought George was going to entertain his cousins and show off with a couple of thrusts at his special dartboard over the sink ... but that was not on his agenda.

George slowly moved over against Mr. Poole, who stood at the cash register taking care of a customer. Poole was now facing the hallway and waiting for the next customer. Without a word of warning, George moved in and pinned Mr. Poole against the counter's edge with the left side of his body. George ran his left hand down the right side of Poole's pant leg until he felt a bulge, gripped the knot and pulled it away from Poole's leg, and with one swift, sweeping motion he sliced off the whole pocket from the man's pant leg and threw it up on the counter. Money rolled every which way on the floor. Mr. Poole had been at work for only a few hours and he had pinched a roll of quarters and a handful of loose quarters, a roll of dimes, two twenty-dollar bills, and a bunch of dollar bills. As far as I saw, no words were exchanged. However, both men broke out into immediate sobs.

Mr. Poole skedaddled and ran off the pier, with people taking double peeks at his tears and the strange-looking outfit he was wearing. George did not speak for a few minutes' time, and when he did speak he announced he was going home. It was plain to see that George was crushed. He was so heartbroken, he cried to find out that his good friend was a common crook. They all left and I had to work a few more hours, until Ann sent young Harvey Nippins to relieve me. I was terribly shaken with the drama of the midday scene. His tears made me realize that George's heart was really broken. However, I was relieved that George's mood did not command him to commit a serious crime. After all, Dick Poole was his longtime best friend, which friendship was now at a complete and final end. Clearly, George was sickened over finding this out, but he showed no murderous or dangerous attitudes.

Not only did I hope that "goddamn leak" had ended, I knew it ended that very day.

ٮ

40 – Rhonda's Rule

    This was going to be my last year with Bone's Pier. Linwood and I had contracted with the Runk Construction Company to have our retirement cottage built on a high treed lot on a quiet street down in quaint old St. Augustine, a half-hour's drive southward. We had enjoyed living for ten years in the Martin Williams (no relation to the pier builder) townhouse complex on Thirteenth Avenue S. and Second Street, Jax Beach, but the rent was escalating fifty dollars a month every year, and since my husband's recent retirement we thought it was best to stabilize our living expenses since we were now going to live on a fixed income.
    Another reason to move was because Jax Beach was becoming too doggone dangerous due to the riffraff moving into our neighborhood. We were renting in a brand-new building, but this immediate area was full of old summer houses, shanties, and bungalows which became occupied by gangs of motorcyclists who were into their own way of life, noisy and riotous. They ganged up and met beside our building, and roared off on a holiday every weekend. This district had changed drastically in the past ten years.
    In our absence, our house was entered and ransacked, as were those of some of our immediate neighbors'. The convenience store, across the street and through the alley on Route A1A, was being robbed frequently. The cars on our street were broken into regularly, the windshields (yes, ours too) were smashed on every car parked on the same block. The police were busy people, rushing back and forth across town with their sirens screaming all night long. The nearby Joe's Bar and Grill, on Sixteenth Avenue S. at the ocean, was officially shut down due to incidents involving numerous live ammunition encounters. We needed less excitement in our retirement and St. Augustine beckoned us away.

…

In the meantime we continued to fish for our enjoyable seafood, and I kept working part-time on the pier. Only now, I had a different boss. Ms. Rhonda was in charge of operations. What a beautiful change, to see the pier business conducted in a professional way. She made immediate repairs on the pier-house. Also, some new pylons were installed to support sections of the pier, to satisfy the requirements of the Army Corps of Engineers who examined the facility regularly.

The pier had a quiet hallway these days because George was restricted to keep himself in low key to please his "ever trying" daughter. He fished a lot more lately, and he joyously attended to work needed on the pier itself. Using his carpentry skills he rebuilt new cleaning tables and repaired the intercom system. Business was good on fair days and not so good on cold or rainy days. But that is how it always was with the fishing pier.

I began to hear about a rift going on between Mrs. Ann Bone and the restaurant people. It seemed the lessees were asking for more than the owners were able to provide. They didn't even consult George for anything anymore. They were requesting things from the women. They demanded that their restrooms be refurbished with modern urinals, toilets, and sinks, and the kitchen be entirely reengineered. When they were informed this was not an immediate possibility, the relationship turned sour. Arty and Farty began to act up unpleasantly.

The first thing I noticed was that they were acting unfriendly towards George, no longer offering him free coffee and instead presenting him with a check whenever he entered the restaurant for a cup of java. I don't think this bothered George because he was always willing to pay. George was not a man who needed to be given free stuff, though he thought those cups of free coffee were an act of friendliness and he enjoyed that aspect of goodwill.

Then one day Arty actually threw George out of the restaurant. George was attempting to tell them to take it easy with Ann, but made the mistake of using a couple of his favorite expletives in the presence of the sanctimonious ex-officer, who then told George to leave the facility. George had more to say but didn't get the chance. Arty, a tall brute, bodily shoved the smaller George out into the hallway while complaining about George's unpleasant language.

"Get the hell out of my place with your foul mouth!" was Arty's final expression.

Then those restaurant people were responsible for Mrs. George Bone's loss of her driver's license. This was done by directly contacting the motor vehicle department, complaining that they were afraid she was about to kill them or their customers due to her lack of capability to drive safely. The motor vehicle office responded to this grumble and after checking her out they decided they would have to call for her license.

It was true that poor Ann Bone was noticeably crippled from arthritis. She suffered a great deal; we all knew that. Her gnarled hands gave her away immediately, the fingers drawn inward and the knuckles of each joint swollen and pitifully painful. Her condition had worsened a great deal after they moved to live on the brackish waterway in Palm Valley.

One wintry day I stopped by at her shop and found her near tears from the misery in her hands. Her medicine was no longer keeping her free of pain. I asked if I made her a pair of warm flannel mittens, would she wear them as she sat in her shop between customers, and she was quite agreeable to the idea, so I was happy to make the mittens.

We all knew Ann Bone was having trouble with her mobility, but she was a doer and kept doing things as usual. She had to drive or hire someone to haul her about to wholesale houses. As long as she could manage to do it herself, she did her chores well. She knew the time was coming when she would have to hire a chauffeur. But Arty and Farty made that happen before it was a self-decision. They had talked it over, and the fact that makes this tale so ironic is that Farty, the soppy, red-nosed, alcoholic partner, was the guy who went to the authorities with his objections to her driving her car. He told his customers that he felt it was his duty to do this for her benefit.

Rhonda decided to take over the restaurant business and told these fellows that their contract was coming to an end and would not be renewed. Rhonda was soon to be remarried. She and Ronald Robinson had plans that differed from what was going on.

After George retired in 1979 and leased the pier to his daughter, Rhonda eventually improved and renovated every corner and every aspect of the pier business. She began by satisfying the requirements of the city, county, and the Army Corps of Engineers. Rhonda spent $40,000 right off the bat and tightened the pier's stability substantially. The pier was now worth a great deal more as a structure than it was when her father acquired ownership from Mr. Williams back in 1969. The price of real estate had been climbing steadily every year, and especially Florida beach properties.

Rhonda was not one to favor the race tracks. She immediately began to concentrate on making worthwhile improvements so that her customers would want to come back. She chose not to renew the contract with Jake and his partner, and began to run the restaurant business herself, with the help of strong and talented people. Fishermen and women watched as she had the parking lot paved, which I remember held six dozen cars. It was amazing what a difference paving that parking lot made.

Before black hardtop asphalt carpeted the area, the old lot caused many to grumble when people had to carry their cumbersome dropnets, coolers, and fishing gear through the sandy ruts to the pier's wooden boardwalk. The sandy lot was what Mr. Williams used to fondly refer to as the pier's "atmosphere." With Rhonda on the scene, she didn't care what Mr. Williams thought; the pier's environment was taking on a more modern mode.

The Jacksonville Beach City Council renewed the pier's franchise after Rhonda installed a new roof over the pier-house. She repainted and remodeled the restaurant and put in new fixtures, added some new furniture and ceiling fans, and redressed the old building with new siding. She was proudly thankful for the new season's onslaught of fishermen and women.

The City of Jacksonville Beach, of course, had an interest in this business, for it collected 5 percent of the pier's gross income. In June of 1983, the city's take was advertised to be $1,128.60. That fee would grow even higher in July, August, and September; those hot summer months could be very busy, productive times aboard the pier.

Like her mother, Rhonda's business acumen seemed to grow naturally. Also like her mother, she had a good eye for detail, never forgetting for whom the pier was initially intended. She truly enjoyed the fishermen and women as much as I did, and it was noticeable in her efforts to please each and every one who came to fish on this pier.

At first I thought running the pier might be a dreadful uphill impossibility for her. I thought she was a bit too young; she was in her thirties when she was asked to come home to help run the business. She was exactly the right shot-in-the-behind which this pier badly needed.

Rhonda applied to the Army Corps of Engineers for a permit to rebuild the original 200 feet out into the ocean that the vicious Hurricane Dora carried off at the end of the pier in 1964, when Mr. Williams still owned the facility. This, she knew, would attract more serious fishermen who were interested in reaching more of the larger king mackerel and cobia that traveled in that deeper slough out there.

Rhonda's dream was to expand the restaurant and have live entertainment to please people musically at evening time. She planned to find a talented chef and have tasty exotic seafood on the menu.

"The pier is surrounded by all kinds of surf fishes. Why not make better use of this handy commodity in some way?" she jokingly said to me. I couldn't agree more, because I love stuff like fishcakes and rich, creamy fish chowder similar to that Ed Davis used to make.

Rhonda had recently remarried a gentleman, Ronald Robinson, and together they ran the pier in a businesslike way, keeping up with repairs and adding interesting items to their restaurant menu. Business improved greatly and they were doing quite well.

41 – George Departs

The very first painful jab in Rhonda's heart came in February 1988, when her father died. George Bone had been a fixture on this pier since he arrived as a young man from the Tobacco Belt in North Carolina, seeking construction work, and was hired by Robert L. Williams to build the pier-house and restaurant building on the fishing pier. With Mr. Williams' help, George had been building ever since. He never had fame or riches, but was still in better shape than if he had remained on the farm.

I often wondered how George held on to his business as long as he had, with three major strikes against him: the lack of education; excessive alcohol; and gambling. I have to agree with the cliché that it is better to have tried and lost, than not to have tried at all. There were times when his business was in the blue, and he and Ann were actually a happy couple. I had seen times when I thought there would be a turnaround in George's life, but he chose not to take the road to sobriety.

I know what excessive alcohol demanded of him; that and the dreadful habit of attending the dog tracks so often had taken their toll. For the first few years, George did business without any schooling or preparation other than the guiding hand of Mr. Williams. He did surprisingly well. But his habits separated him from family, as well as from good health, and from his much beloved career as a pier owner. He adored being "the captain of the pier." More than once he told me this fact. He died from heart failure at the age of sixty-three, which we thought was much too young. His family in North Carolina, his disappointing "best friend" Dick Poole, and his gambling broke him down.

And so it was *Sudiev* (Good-bye), farewell, George, it was good to know you.

...

Ten years after Rhonda took over the business, she had a belly full of troubles and was ready to sell the property. She and her husband had been at it for a whole decade and were getting tired of dealing with rising prices and other pressing demands. The cost of labor was growing out of sight and made it difficult for them to maintain good, steady help. When I started working on the pier in 1973 the minimum wage was just under $2.00 per hour; in 1981 it was up to $3.35 per hour, and by 1990 it was $3.80 per hour.

"It's getting tougher and tougher to do the day-to-day things," she complained one morning. "Because of past hurricane winds, insurance rates are going out of sight in Florida. And we've decided that we would rather enjoy doing something else for a change, so I've decided to put the pier up for sale. We don't want to be made old and sick like my parents. Ron and I would like to see Mt. Rushmore, the Grand Canyon, and more of the U.S. of A. while we are still able to travel without a cane," she said with a laugh.

It was plain to see that Rhonda meant business in her declaration to sell out. "The pier is for sale, not for rent and not for leasing; it's for sale to a ready, willing, and able buyer," she declared.

"This pier is in excellent condition, I can say that," boasted Rhonda. "We have been on the ball with its upkeep. It is structurally sound from one end to the other. We've restored everything that needed to be replaced. And every day we check for nails that may loosen and need to be driven down flat to the deck.

"Its purchaser will be able to step right in and enjoy the business and not have to worry about doing a single thing to the structure for some time to come."

Rhonda listed the property with an agency that began to offer the pier to the City of Jacksonville. After all, they argued soundly, tourists coming down from the north were under the impression that Jacksonville is a seaside town, when in reality the city is miles from the Atlantic Ocean. The agency proposed that the city council consider investing in the purchase of this pier to have a tie with its close descendant, Jacksonville Beach. The city's council people thought about it and began to negotiate for the purchase of the pier. For a while it looked promising. Then there followed a period of nerve-racking wrangling, wangling, and a whole lot of whistling in Dixie.

42 – Hurricane Floyd Ends Pier

Then came the big surprise! In September of 1999, Hurricane Floyd blew inshore and dealt Bone's Pier its final blow. When those high winds stopped, the entire pier had suffered extensive damage. It was so bad that the pier had to be closed down. Sadly it sat raggedy and forlorn, and the brokenhearted fishermen had to find other places to fish.

Rhonda finally sold the fractured, weather-twisted structure to Jacksonville's Duval County for $650,000, a fraction of what this beach property was actually worth.

The City of Jacksonville then razed the property that was so long known as Bone's Pier, and they decided to build their own concrete landing farther up, at First Street N., to the tune of several million dollars.

This is the end of my tales concerning the once truly busy Bone's Jax Beach Fishing Pier.

Epilogue

Today there is nothing to see but greenish-blue water where the soul-stirring Bone's Jacksonville Beach Fishing Pier once stood at Sixth Avenue S. and the ocean.

The mighty Atlantic was relatively calm and innocent in appearance when I visited the site forty years later, in 2012. The waves were rolling gently and the seagulls circling overhead squawked as they always had, but they remained secretive as to what they knew concerning this place on this good earth. The once-upon-a-time joy and sadness that this spot had brought to people remains well hidden. As I stood gazing at the space where this active fishing pier was once anchored, I heard many spiritual voices quietly whispering to me. There was much laughter, along with shudders of pain, ascending from the depths of this area of the beach.

At this very spot once was the cypress boardwalk approach to Bone's Jax Beach Fishing Pier. When first built in 1960, the pier was the longest on the Atlantic Coast, stretching 1,200 feet. I could hear its founder, Robert L. Williams, softly weeping in sympathy for the terrifying beating it took from Hurricane Floyd.

I could still hear George Bone's voice speaking on the old intercom: *"Hello, hello, this is your captain. There is a school of menhaden coming our way from the north and they probably have a school of bluefish or Spanish mackerel under them, so be sure to put a fresh bait on your hook and you might catch a fish."*

George so enjoyed giving advice like that. He was always pleased to see his customers catching some kind of seafood.

…

The tradition of pier fishing lives on in Jacksonville, however. A few blocks north of Bone's Pier site, a "new" pier welcomes anglers and spectators alike. The Jacksonville Beach Fishing Pier, at 503 First

Street N., extends nearly a quarter of a mile into the Atlantic Ocean. For information, visit: http://www.jacksonvillebeachpier.com/.

…

The old pier's parking lot is now called Oceanfront Park, one of the city of Jacksonville Beach's recreational areas complete with sizable sculptures. Shaded by tall palm trees, these shapes depict a huge snake and tortoise for children to hug and climb upon. Weather-proofed boxes containing informative posters surround the park, explaining the area's sea oats, seashells, shorebirds, and things that sometimes are seen when watching the ocean, such as migrating right whales, porpoises, and sea turtles.

In the center of the main pathway is a unique bronze sculpture named "Sea Express," created by Kristen Visbal. It depicts a life-size teenage boy joyfully riding atop a jolly little bottlenose dolphin. The boy's countenance clearly shows viewers he is having a wonderful time. Although I failed to see how this tableau is supposed to represent the future of the city, the emotion of pleasure is portrayed artfully well on both figures.

Also while there, I noticed the ever-changing neighborhood. Many of the old-time summer cottages surrounding the area, which once housed noisy motorcycle gangs when I was there throughout the 1970s and into the 1980s, are now gone from the scene. Most of these ancient dwellings were replaced with modern high-rise, high-priced condominiums. First Street was quiet; we heard no annoying roaring sounds.

The place where Bone's Jax Beach Fishing Pier once proudly stood is now but a memory. Only the breezes from the unpredictable trade winds whisper unidentifiable plans into our ears.

At this spot was the cypress boardwalk approach to the Bone's Jax Beach Fishing Pier. It stretched over the Atlantic Ocean for 1,200 feet.

A sculpture named "The Sea Express," by Kristen Visbal, marks the site of the former Bone's Jax Beach Pier.

Recipes

These tackle shop recipes were so enjoyed that we thought we'd share them with others.

WONDRA'S FLORIDA FOLK CAKE

1 scant cup orange juice
1 cup brown sugar
1 orange
1 cup raisins
1/3 cup oil
1 cup sugar
1 cup buttermilk
2 eggs
2 cups flour
1 teaspoon baking soda
1 teaspoon salt
1/4 teaspoon white pepper

Our method:
1. Squeeze orange juice. Mix the brown sugar with juice and set aside.
2. Grind the whole orange with the peel (without seeds, though), along with the raisins. To this, add the oil, sugar, buttermilk, and eggs.
3. Sift the flour, soda, salt, and pepper together, and add to the buttermilk mixture and beat together.
4. Bake in a 9" x 13" pan at 375 degrees F for 33 minutes.
5. Immediately pour the orange juice and brown sugar over the entire cake.
6. Serve hot or cold. It is even better with whipped cream.

(For your next party, try our)
PARTY RED BEANS

4 lbs. dried red beans (two packs of 2 lbs. each)
2 teaspoons baking soda
1 ham bone with some meat, or 2 lbs. of smoked ham
2 tablespoons brown sugar
2 tablespoons honey
5 or 6 bay leaves
½ cup Creole seasoning
1 teaspoon salt
1/2 teaspoon white pepper
1/3 cup corn or vegetable oil
2 large onions, chopped
1/2 cup garlic cloves, minced
1 cup green pepper, chopped
1 cup fresh celery, chopped

Our method:

Put red beans and soda in a large stockpot and generously cover with water. Let soak overnight.

Next day, drain the soak water off and cover the beans with fresh, cool water to two inches above the beans. Add the ham, sugar, honey, bay leaves, Creole seasoning, salt, and white pepper.

In a large frypan, place the oil, onions, and garlic, and sauté until the onions and garlic are sweated and opaque. Then add this and the green pepper and celery to the bean pot and turn up the burner. When beans are up to boiling, turn down the heat to where beans are gently simmering. Simmer until the beans are tender and creamy, not less than one hour.

Ed served his red beans over a scoop of white rice, along with slices of smoked ham or sausage.

Serves 12–15 people.

With this dish, women like red wine and men prefer beer.

VANILLA CREAM CHEESE PIE
(was a favorite at the tackle shop)

1 package (3-1/4 ounces) vanilla pudding mix
2 cups whole milk
1 package (8 ounces) cream cheese (any brand)
1 teaspoon vanilla
1 8-inch prepared graham cracker pie crust
a couple dozen dead-ripe strawberries, hulled, rinsed, and dried
1 pint freshly picked blueberries, rinsed, and dried
vanilla ice cream or any other topping

Mix pudding mix and milk in a saucepan and bring to a full rolling boil, stirring constantly with a wooden spoon. When fully thickened, remove from heat and add cream cheese and stir until well blended and smooth. Add the vanilla, and let mixture cool, stirring it several times.

When cooled, pour pudding into the crust and refrigerate at least a couple of hours or even overnight. Then decorate the pie by placing strawberries in a circle around the edge of the pudding. Pour blueberries over the center top of the pudding.

We served it with a dollop of ice cream or whipped cream and watched to see how many servings George and Richard would have, since they lusted for this delicious dessert.

BEER-BATTER FISH FRY

2-1/2 lbs. of fish (about six or eight medium blue, or any medium-sized fish fillets)
1 cup flour
1 egg yolk
1/3 cup beer
1/2 teaspoon salt
1/3 cup milk
1/4 cup cold water
1 egg white

Place flour in a mixing bowl and add the egg yolk, beer, and salt, and mix well. Set aside. Combine the milk and water, and add about a third at a time to the flour mixture, beating well each addition until batter is smooth. Let the batter rest a few minutes. Beat the egg white until frothy and add this to the batter just before ready to sauté. Dip the fish fillets into the batter and fry until golden brown on both sides.

A QUICK FISH REPAST

4 to 6 medium-sized fillets (such as whiting, pompano, blues, sheepshead, etc.)
1 large ripe tomato, diced
1 cup celery (cut only 1-inch long)
1 large, firm green pepper (sliced or julienned)
2 large cloves of garlic, finely chopped
1 medium-sized onion, chopped into small pieces
3 tablespoons fresh parsley, finely chopped
1/2 teaspoon salt
1/2 teaspoon black pepper
1-1/2 cups cracker or bread crumbs
3 to 4 tablespoons melted butter
1/2 teaspoon white pepper
1/2 cup parmesan cheese (or any other choice)
1/2 teaspoon paprika

Our method:

Preheat oven to 400 degrees F. Combine tomato, celery, green pepper, garlic, and onion, and spread over bottom of a casserole pan. Place fillets over the vegetables and sprinkle with most of the fresh parsley (save a little), and season with salt and black pepper. Combine crumbs, butter, white pepper, parmesan cheese, and paprika, and spread evenly over fish and pack down around fish.

Bake 15–20 minutes, until fish flakes when pierced with a fork.

Sprinkle with fresh parsley and serve over grits, rice, or mashed potatoes.

APPLE FRITTERS
(one of George's favorite treats)

1 large egg
2/3 cup milk
1-1/3 cups flour
2 teaspoons baking powder
1/4 teaspoon salt
1/4 teaspoon nutmeg
4 to 5, any choice, cooking apples (coarsely grated or chopped)

Our method:
    In a large bowl, beat egg and milk together, and add flour, baking powder, salt, and nutmeg, and mix together. Add the grated apple and mix into the batter. Fry tablespoon-sized fritters in medium-hot pan, with any oil of choice. When golden brown, turn over and fry until golden brown. Place fritters onto a platter with double sheets of paper towels to collect any excess oil.
    Dust the fritter with powdered sugar, and serve hot or cold.

OUR PIER'S CRAB CAKES

1 pound or so of cooked and picked blue crab meat
1 egg
3 green onions, finely chopped
3 tablespoons fresh parsley, chopped
2 tablespoons Dijon-style mustard
1 teaspoon Old Bay Seasoning
1 tablespoon Worcestershire Sauce
3/4 cup thick white sauce (made with 3 tablespoons butter, 3 tablespoons flour, and 3/4 cup milk)

Ingredients for coating the cakes:
1/3 cup flour, mixed with 1/2 teaspoon Old Bay Seasoning
1 well-beaten egg
1 cup pulverized soda crackers

Our method:
    Put shell-free crabmeat into a sizable bowl and add in the seven following ingredients and mix well. Cool mixture in the refrigerator for an hour or so. With hands, make 6 or 8 cakes of equal size. Dip each cake into first the flour, then into the beaten egg, and finally into the cracker meal, and fry in medium-hot oil of choice, about 3 minutes each side, until golden brown. Add additional oil if needed.
    Serve with a wedge of lemon and a glass of sweetened iced tea.

About the Author

A great-grandmother, Eve Bates has announced her fourth literary project, *The Pier: Glimpses of My Exotic Life on Bone's Jax Beach Fishing Pier, 1972–1983*. This pier proved to be where she witnessed many auspicious events.

Her first book, *Sudiev! Good-bye!: Joys and Hardships of a Lithuanian Immigrant Girl* (a parental biography), has a permanent home at the Statue of Liberty Museum Library at Ellis Island, New York. Her two other books, collections of eclectic short stories, are titled *My Speckled Tales and Other Dimensions* and *More Speckled Tales*.

Eve Bates transformed her life from the child of immigrant tomato growers to that of a sophisticated traveler. She has been to most continents and major cities of the world. Her travels began when she married Linwood Tomlinson Bates, a Hamilton watch salesman, and together they attended his international sales meetings.

She remembers a wonderful childhood on a Burlington, New Jersey, farm. Eve has enjoyed a fulfilling life as a wife, a mother of two and grandmother of three, and finally, as a writer and storyteller. She maintains a membership with the Tale Tellers of St. Augustine, Florida, who recount their marvelous stories in schools, churches, and theaters.

The author hopes you'll find *The Pier*'s strange characters as engaging as she did.